POWER TALK

POWER TALK

USING LANGUAGE TO BUILD AUTHORITY AND INFLUENCE

SARAH MYERS McGINTY, Ph.D.

WARNER BOOKS

A Time Warner Company

Warner Books, Inc., 1271 Avenue of the Americas, New York, NY 10020
Visit our Web site at www.twbookmark.com
W A Time Warner Company

Printed in the United States of America
First Printing: February 2001
10 9 8 7 6 5 4 3 2 1

Library of Congress Cataloging-in-Publication Data
McGinty, Sarah Myers.
    Power talk: using language to build authority and influence / Sarah Myers McGinty.
    p. cm.
    Includes bibliographical references.
    ISBN: 0-446-52537-5
    1. Business communication. I. Title.
HF5718 M433 2001
658.4'52—dc21   00-044932

Book design by Giorgetta Bell McRee

To the boys on the team and the girl who coached

ACKNOWLEDGMENTS

When readers ask writers, "Is this book about you?," the answer has to be "Yes!" While the exact relationship between the written product and the author remains inscrutable—even to the writer herself—everything in this book connects to what I've seen and thought, done and imagined, heard and listened for. Done properly, the naming of resources would be an impossible task.

Here, then, it must be done improperly. Acknowledging the inevitable omissions, I thank for their immediate and direct help my able, patient, and enthusiastic editor Rob McMahon, as well as Ethan Kline, Rafe Sagalyn, Geoff Colvin, and Justin Martin. The Expository Writing Program and the Teacher Education Program at Harvard, as well as the staff at Lamont and Baker libraries, have been important in this work. My research assistant, Debra Grossman, kept me on track, and I received invaluable research support from Pat Bellanca, Sarah N. McGinty, John E. McGinty, Ann Holby, and Christopher Conroy. Other important contributors were Charlotte Sibley, Patti

Hunt Dirlam, Karen Kemby, Sharon Kellogg, Herminia lbarra, Robin Wagner, Amy Kautzman, Ross Wood, Steve Sayers, Judith Heller, Judy Bidwell, Bill Crowley, Andy Walter, Melinda McGinty, Karen Stevenson, Rhonda Davis Smith, Phil Driscoll, Sig Heller, Curtis Hartman, Sam Chwat, Nancy Boardman, Dan Hoffman, Caroline O'Neill, Mike and Claudia Thornburgh, sales personnel at Creative Office Pavilion, Michael Schu, Joe Fennewald, and the coxes and oarsmen of the Harvard crew. The inspiration of fellow scholars, especially Virginia Valian, cannot pass without mention.

CONTENTS

A Note about Notes

Knowledge does not stand alone. All ideas and insights develop within the context of the work of other researchers, thinkers, and writers. This book is no exception, and while it is not meant to be an academic textbook, it nonetheless draws on and references the work of other scholars. I have followed the convention of trade books and do not footnote within the text; I direct you to the Notes at the end, where my sources are cited. You will find a Bibliography there as well, offering direction for follow-up reading where a topic or idea interests you.

INTRODUCTION

So how are things at work?

- Does your boss overlook your contributions? Does your team ignore your ideas? Do your colleagues forget your suggestions?
- Do you struggle to create consensus in your department?
- Are you headed for a new company or a new location?
- Are the skills you need for the next position different from those you mastered in entry-level work?
- Are you on the fast track with a plan or stalled on the shoulder without a clue?

If your answer is yes to any (or many) of these questions, this book was written for you. Work is about performance. But performance—what you've done, where you've succeeded, and who knows about it—depends on your ability to communicate. How can I make the most of the time I have to talk? How can I persuade others to follow my plan? How can I be sure my

1

ideas are remembered as mine? How can I create authority? How can I inspire collaboration? Speech and language choices figure into all these situations, and they are as important to the solutions as good ideas or an impressive title. Yes, work is about performance, but recognition and promotion require good communication skills.

Good communication skills required. Every job posting lists good communication skills as a necessary qualification. But what are good communication skills? A loud voice? An extensive vocabulary? The power to persuade? The stylistic flair of a poet? We often assume communication skills aren't much more than the ability to write a clear memo or pull together an efficient agenda. But spoken language, rather than writing, is at the heart of most business communication. Talk is how we prefer to do business. We feel inefficient and frustrated when the workday is full of messaging options, voice mail, telephone tag, and the black hole of holding. We want to talk to people directly, explain ourselves, practice our own brand of chatter and charm. While memos, e-mails, reports, and letters all convey important information, the relationships we create and the impressions we convey are built on what we say and how we say it.

Specialists find that presentation speakers have about thirty seconds to capture the attention of an audience. Isn't that true every time we open our mouths? As the most constant way we interact with each other, speech conveys our ideas, intelligence, and values. But it also conveys our assurance, confidence, and leadership. These factors, as well as the work we do, get us hired, adopted as a protégé, or promoted. Appearance may be the first thing people notice, but initial impressions are quickly undercut (or overcome) by words. Speech choices create power and influence.

Good communication skill, as defined in this book, is an understanding of how situation shapes speech and how speech shapes situation. It has nothing to do with proper grammar, accents, vocabulary lessons, or the gerund. Rather, the agenda here is subversive: a look behind the scenes, a chance to examine the speech conventions of our world—the sociology of language—as a means to understanding, competence, and control. Such a behind-the-scenes view complicates understanding, but it also creates intentional (and thus more effective) speech choices. Think of the photocopying machine in the back office. You know how to make copies. But if you know something more—how it works, how to change the toner, how to clear a jam—you have real control of the tool. A higher level of understanding puts you ahead of the guy who only knows how to hit the print button. Understanding speech styles and the forces that affect those styles is an advantage in the workplace far beyond what you get from fixing a back office machine. It can give you thirty seconds more airtime in a meeting, help you stave off the assaults others make on your speech moments, build your authority, and enhance your credibility and impact.

Speech awareness even supports the transition to a new position or to a new employer. You can sound like a divisional head, a VP, a manager, or a supervisor while you're learning to be one; language allows you to borrow authority from words while expertise and experience accumulate. Student teachers, for example, begin September with a few stock phrases and spend the rest of the year learning to teach. They manage with "All right, people, let's settle down" and "This is due tomorrow" as they develop skills, strategies, and a personal style of teaching. Emily was a particular favorite. Her background was in improvisational theater. She had a special advantage because she knew, at least to begin with, it was going to be a bit of an act, a matter of *sounding* right until she learned the job!

"Hold on!" you say. "I've been talking all my life. I don't need anyone to show me how to do this. At the age of two, I set off with a firm command of 'Da-da' and the rest is history!"

Actually, that's part of the problem. Since we all began talking without formal instruction, very little of our education focused on speech and language study. There was some sentence diagramming in seventh grade and vocabulary drilling in eleventh. When you joined your firm, you learned industry buzzwords like ebitda, wacc, or double nickels. You uncon-

3

sciously adopted the shorthand language for the product line and the client roster. But the sociology of language—how social forces and speech patterns interact—wasn't part of either your school curriculum or your corporate training program.

Several other forces make it easy to overlook this discipline and the ways that social and situational forces affect conversation and communication. One is the fact that language learning is largely unconscious. It hardly seems necessary to offer instruction. As George Bernard Shaw's Eliza Doolittle declares in estimating the price of lessons from speech specialist Henry Higgins: "You wouldn't have the face to ask me the same for teaching me my own language as you would for French; so I won't give more than a shilling." Our own facility with language, the competence we achieved before we even went to school, makes speech instruction seem no more necessary than breathing lessons.

And precisely because you have been talking all your life, you probably don't know what you really sound like or how you choose the words you use. My student Adam, a life-long resident of Long Island, confessed to me that he was in high school before he realized that many people pronounced the nearby airport, La Guardia, with an "r" sound in the middle. For fifteen years, he had never consciously heard anyone say anything but "Lagwadia" and he assumed that somehow this word had a silent r in the middle of it. In college, he was surprised that his friends teased him about his pronunciation: "I felt like this was my airport—I lived ten minutes from the runways—and *they* were telling *me* how to pronounce it?!" What we do know about speech, and especially about our own speech, was learned unsystematically. Our own daily familiarity with our speech choices inhibits analysis. We often hear ourselves clearly only through the ears of someone else . . . and we can be surprised by what they hear.

To complicate matters, language and identity are strongly connected. The sound of our speech is part of how we know who we are. A sub, a hero, or a grinder? A bucket or a pail? A faucet or a spigot? Catty-corner, caddy-corner, or caddywumpus? Whatever you've grown up saying seems "right." The transplanted speaker who suppresses her "Lagwadia" or "y'all" or "thee-*ay*-ter" finds it all comes back on the phone to Dad or at Grandma's dinner table. Words tell us when we're home.

We are, in part, then, what we say. We draw identity from our speech habits. The power of the Québécois in Canada, the controversy over the recognition of Black Vernacular English in Oakland, California, the resistance of the Académie to Americanisms in French, prove that language and identity are intertwined in profound and complicated ways. Our speech habits may only occasionally be the object of direct study or awareness, but when they are held up to the light, tempers flare, dictionaries are hauled out, and most of us vow that our beloved pronunciation is the only one, our favorite phrase the most apt, our name for a thing the name God intended. Thus, because we are first unconscious of our own ways of saying things—remember the first time you heard your voice played back on a tape recorder?—and next because we tend to cling to and defend our words and ways, the effort to acquire more objective ears is difficult. But an understanding of the forces that shape speech choices and the impact of those choices is an essential communication skill. This understanding makes the unconscious conscious, the accidental intentional. It offers flexibility and control. And it underlies power and influence.

The good news is that this isn't going to be like learning statistics or passing the CFA or mastering Dutch. Remember the "Da-da" days. You were a first-rate talker at four. And since then, you've nimbly adapted to the expanded vocabulary of school and work, the constant changes of language convention. Are you saying "Whazzup?" or "So there you go" or "It's all about . . . "? Have you noticed that "Do me a favor" now precedes a reprimand rather than a request? Do you have some "concerns" about all this? (We're delivering our criticisms as "concerns" these days.) Are we "on the same page"? We need to be. And by the way, watch out for that word "need." It's started to mean "should."

" WAHHHZUP?"

You: "What's the deadline for the Zimmerman report?"
Your boss: "You need to get that to me by Friday."

It looks like a late night for you on Thursday. But *you* don't need to get some annoying report done by Friday. Your boss just made *her* need into yours! It's amazing how easily and how unconsciously we adapt to language's change and vitality.

So read on with confidence. *Power Talk* is the advanced course for speakers looking for more control of their words and their impact. Language's sneaky habit of constant change is already a part of your life; what lies before you has nothing to do with diagramming sentences. In fact, the organized study of the intersections of speech and social convention is more like psychology or sociology than high school grammar. When we dabble in sociolinguistics, when we raise to the level of consciousness important judgments and strategies in our speech exchanges, we sort out the influence of situation on speech.

And we observe how language contributes to that situation. Knowing which words sound like power, both the direct power of authority and the indirect power of influence, is more useful than spelling skills or PowerPoint. Such knowledge lets you showcase your ideas and take your performance public.

Of course, language doesn't create reality. Excellent work—top sales figures, long hours, innovative programs, new accounts—comes first. But excellent work is uncovered in conversations, broadcast in phone calls, hyped in meetings, and shared through spoken communication. All day long, we create power and credibility with our performance, with work *and* words. Understanding how language shapes situation gives you greater control of the situation. It provides a workbox of useful tools and a way to think about language choices that can change minds and increase options. An informed and thorough knowledge of language, free from subjectivity and false ideas about correctness or difference, can help you speak with wiser intention, listen with greater insight, and judge others with more equity. If you will cross-examine your own speech style, the world you work in, and the situations you struggle with, you can strengthen your own position and make good use of your successes (and failures). Some of these successes and failures will hinge on components of communication and some won't. But study of the sociology of speech will multiply your communication options and give you access to power and influence that might otherwise elude you. This knowledge is true power.

Herewith, then, a user's guide to language. Predicated on the belief that language is power and that knowledge of language is a political tool, this book will take a skill you already have—speech—and show you how to make the most of it. With an understanding of the relationship between power and language, you can accurately analyze speech situations, gain control over the impression you create, convey the right message, and accomplish your goals. This book will show you how to use your knowledge of language to create power and influence.

Chapter One

Language from the Center

Getting to the top of any given mountain was considered much less important than *how* one got there: prestige was earned by tackling the most unforgiving routes with minimal equipment, in the boldest style imaginable.

JONATHAN KRAKAUER, *Into Thin Air*

Like any thrown-together group—a pickup basketball game, a rowboat full of survivors, an ad hoc committee planning the annual company picnic—the eight people who tumbled out of the hotel's minivan for the "scenic trail hike" had different styles, values, and expectations for the day. Jerry was determined to demonstrate how experienced he was. Hector was committed to being jolly. Lynn was there to burn calories. Dana was there for the views. Alyse, a city dweller, and Walter, who had recently had knee surgery, were worried that they might not be able to keep up. Jack and Harold were focused on lenses, apertures, light levels, and film speed. To make this a successful experience, the hotel had assigned the group two guides, Claire and Sheila. Claire led the pack up the hill. Sheila brought up the rear. The two stayed in contact throughout the day with walkie-talkies and occasional conversations when the group paused to rest, eat, or reconsider the route.

Claire and Sheila agreed that both their jobs were important, but the hikers in general looked upon Claire as the leader of the hike, the guide in charge. Jerry and Lynn hung out with Claire. The more experienced hikers sat with her on breaks. Claire checked the route, made decisions, and set the pace. Alyse, Walter, and Hector hung out with Sheila. Sheila kept the stragglers going; she motivated and encouraged the slower hikers, she accommodated the talkers who wanted to chatter rather than climb, and she dealt with the inexperienced, the injured, and the out-of-condition. Claire's seemed like the important work, although Sheila's was probably just as difficult.

Throughout the day, Claire's role as declared leader was reflected in her speech style:

"Remember to pace yourselves for the whole day."
"You need to be drinking water at least every mile."
"We can't take that route and be back before sunset."
"I know . . . that looks interesting . . . but there's a drop-off and the creek was too deep to cross yesterday. We'll take a different route to the summit."

Claire's language style inspired confidence in her group. When she said the route was closed, that settled it. And if she found the pace too fast or too slow, the hikers made the proper adjustments. No one knew if Claire was highly experienced; none of the hikers had ever met her before. But through her speech style, she was able to gain the confidence and the trust of her group, and they listened to what she told them.

When we speak, we often choose to be either Claire or Sheila. We choose to lead or to encourage. Certainly, both styles are important because each has its own advantages and disadvantages. This chapter, however, looks at Language from the Center, the language habits and speech markers that sound like leadership and aim for control.

WHAT LANGUAGE FROM THE CENTER SOUNDS LIKE

1. Directs Rather Than Responds
2. Makes Statements
3. Contextualizes with Authority
4. Contradicts, Argues, and Disagrees
5. Practices Affect of Control

WHAT LANGUAGE FROM THE CENTER CONVEYS

Language from the Center, like Claire, takes the lead. It suggests competence and confident familiarity. The speaker is knowledgeable, working comfortably in familiar territory; since he's been here or done this before, we can trust him. There aren't going to be any unpleasant surprises. Language from the Center makes a speaker sound like a leader.

LANGUAGE FROM THE CENTER SOUNDS LIKE COMPETENCE, KNOWLEDGE, AND AUTHORITY

Donna Demizio wants to talk to you about your desk. For the last eleven years, Demizio has sold the workstations and design services of Office Creations, the largest contract furniture dealer in New England. Her knowledge of desks, chairs, cubicles, partitions, pedestals, lighting, and laterals has helped Demizio average about five million dollars a year for OC over the last four years. This year—it's only September—she's written up six million dollars.

11

Demizio gets to the office at 7:00 A.M. and checks her mailbox: five hand-written messages and six faxes. Not bad, she thinks. She heads to her desk and logs on to e-mail: eighteen messages. Okay—with luck, that's half an hour's work. Next, her voice mail, which can warehouse up to twenty messages. It's full. The first message: "Donna—it's Adrienne at PYC—listen, the caster just fell off my file puppy—can you deal with this for me—it's an emergency 'cuz I can't even get the drawers open with the thing lying here like it's got a flat tire—thanks, kiddo." By the time Demizio has done the rough triage on the messages, noted the important numbers, and shuttled whatever she can to someone else's desk, it's 8:30 A.M. and she's already behind for her first client, the one that doesn't have adjacent parking. It looks like it's going to be one of those days.

While she's driving, Demizio returns phone calls. She tries to prioritize, but every client wants immediate attention. She completes her first appointment, a law firm looking to reconfigure support staff space, and then heads downtown to her top client, New England Bank. Time to check her beeper and phone in for messages. She can't make important calls from the car and risk getting cut off in the middle of a delicate negotiation or a pitch—she liked the Central Artery better when it wasn't a tunnel—but she can leave her own cluster of follow-up messages, play phone tag to keep connected to her accounts, and do some of the baby-sitting that constitutes 75 percent of her work. Today she'll have to be a farmer, giving her time and energy to existing accounts, seeding for the future with established clients, and keeping people happy with follow-up contact. But she needs time to be a hunter, too. Looking for leads, keeping up with the churn, researching the influential decision-makers is tough to do on the run.

By the end of the day, Demizio has seen five clients, made thirty-five phone calls, sent forty-one e-mails, been paged eight times, checked her voice messages five times, and sent or received fifteen faxes. She's checked in with all twenty-four of her active clients and made brief contact with at least six more on her list. She's promised herself for the third time not to cut the next leads group breakfast. And she's told Eric, her account coordinator, to send a new 1488845-01 caster to Adrienne.

Demizio's speech style is assured and sometimes even aggressive. As a seasoned salesperson, she knows the business and she knows her product down to the smallest specification. Her clients typically think little about where their work occurs. So Demizio's initial contacts with companies are mostly informational. She describes product lines, bats around space configurations, and explains different price points. The next round of conversations will be educational as well: quality versus remanufactured product, current design trends, multiple applications for product, spatial flexibility for the future. Somewhere along the line, she must explain that vendors no longer stock inventory. Thus every job is fully customized—even if the core of the order is common components—and every job takes longer than the client figured.

When the client agrees to a presentation—has visited the showroom, reviewed the catalogues, accepted the time line—Demizio organizes a sales presentation involving CAD drawings, specifications, pricing, and little squares of fabric the size of playing cards. Months of conversation, negotiation, and necessary sign-offs may follow. Demizio, on the phone, at the fax, at the job site throughout this time, works to create (on a time line that from day one was unrealistically short) an affordable match between the clients' needs and the products she represents. Some of her meetings are binder dumps in a conference room. Some of her contacts are just electronic dart games of close-but-not-quite communication. Once in a while she has time to uncover the aesthetic and conceptual issues behind a project. Mostly she's "maxed out" and a little cynical about the latest Customer Intimacy Initiative. As Demizio sees it, the bulk of her job is the delivery of information and the education of her clients. But service and solutions get complicated in the two-way squeeze between impatient planners who can't afford the downtime of spatial reorganization and unreliable vendors with nothing in stock. Demizio works entirely on commission. She, too, is in a hurry and behind every day of the month. Language from the Center seems like the right way to stay even.

1. DIRECTS RATHER THAN RESPONDS

Demizio directs rather than responds in most of her conversations. She interprets her projects to the design and implementation teams, leaving highly specific voice mail messages that begin "I need you to . . ." And she guides her clients in the selection of what seem like chairs and desks to her and like mission statements and employee satisfaction to them. She has a lot to say.

When New England Bank decided to downsize and reorganize its business marketing group into cross-functional teams, the workspace had to change. Looking for new configurations of employees, offering new products and services, NEB came back to the same company that had sold them lobby furniture when they upgraded the entrance to their executive offices on the thirty-sixth floor. Demizio gave her careful attention to that project—eight chairs, two tables, and a $9,000 combination desk/credenza. Now NEB needs a solution for eight thousand square feet of offices, conference rooms, and interactive work zones. New England Bank hasn't made a substantial furniture purchase in seven years and the present computer network, internal e-mail system, phone, and video-conferencing setup mean that new technology, as well as the new sociology of the department, figure in the plans. Demizio is invited to bid on the project.

Michael Scheff, NEB's facilities manager, is a familiar contact and a good buddy. Demizio drops off the binders depicting OC's furniture lines the day after Scheff calls. She has several conversations with Scheff over the next week and does most of her listening over the phone before she prepares materials for a meeting with the planners. She meets with an OC project manager and with OC designers to prepare for her pitch. She rereads research on team types compiled by one of

14

her suppliers and photocopies two preliminary sketches from ZAccess, her design software program. By the time she arrives at NEB, she's a walking encyclopedia. To complicate matters, the NEB people haven't thought much about how their new team concept is going to work on a daily basis; they only know it's what the consultant recommended. Having committed themselves to the concept and announced the reengineering idea, management wants to put the new layout in place as soon as possible. Before the meeting, Demizio reminds herself to listen carefully. But she is also aware that no one sees this project as a particularly fun thing to do. Just necessary. She needs to convey a lot of information fast, including the fact that this isn't going to be done next week. She figures if she can sound knowledgeable about product and process, she can simplify their decision and clinch the job.

> Purchasing manager: "Management is focusing on a new work style here but I think cost-reduction is also a top priority."
>
> Division head: "We want flexibility . . . the projects are going to change and so will the setup of the teams. But we need this yesterday."
>
> Demizio: "Okay . . . good . . . I hear you . . . let's look at these sketches I worked up on ZAccess. I want to walk you through my first thoughts and I can show you some of the different lines and pricing. Then we can talk about lead-time issues and installation options. If you'll look at page six of the handout, you'll see five principles of team organization . . ." [uh-oh, the division head just checked his watch].

Language from the Center, language that directs rather than responds, is Demizio's logical choice. She will talk longer and talk more than other speakers in the room. She manages this conversation, initiates the topics, and sets the real agenda of the hour. She may need to enforce her agenda, too, redirecting the conversation when necessary, moving attention away from management's vision to the number of desks, the number of network connections, or the number of windows on the north side of the building. Here Demizio works from the Center, dominating as the presenter to NEB's people.

Demizio paces the meeting as well, moving on, cutting off a line of inquiry; returning to a key point with statements like "Let's get back to our first concern . . ." or "That's an interesting point but I think we need to stick with . . . ," Demizio functions as the gatekeeper. At this presentation meeting with planners, she must deliver specific information about materials, specifications, service, and cost. She will probably have to ask the group to back up several times. And she will attempt to keep the conversation on topics that highlight the strengths of OC. But while she will try to appear responsive, she is directing the conversation as much here as in her own internal team meetings. With her OC account manager, project manager, designer, and installation people, she also has a lot of information to convey, a lot to say, and limited time. In both settings, her language is directive; she leads her listeners where she thinks they need to go.

Language from the Center relies on more than taking the floor, however, and on more than directive statements and airtime. The speaker must also be able to hold the floor. With Language from the Center, the speaker feels authorized to recapture or change the conversational flow. This redirection can be accomplished, as Demizio did above, with transitional sentences that refocus the conversation: "Let's look at these. . . ." It can also be accomplished by interruption, a factor in most fast-paced conversations. Sociologist Erving Goffman, who with linguists like William Labov brought sociology, psychology, and linguistics together in new intersections of study, found plenty of interruption when speakers feel comfortable with one another. The little break-ins were not experienced as attacks on the turf of topic. Some were, in fact, affirmations. The listener who nods may throw in a "That's right." He isn't interrupting; he's actually reinforcing the conversational direction.

Purchasing manager: "And finally, we need to talk about desk heights. . . ."
Demizio: "Absolutely."

When overlap falls near the speaker's natural conclusion, this interruption suggests involvement, rather than redirection. Researchers Candace West and Don Zimmerman demonstrated in several studies of both acquainted and unacquainted speakers that interruption timed to fall at the perceived end of a speaker's point does not redirect but builds on the existing conversation.

The interruption of Language of the Center, however, is not the affirmative or bonding interruption. It is corrective, a redirection of the topic, a claim on the conversational turf.

Purchasing manager: "We need to talk about the desk heights and whether . . ."
Demizio: "We can give you anything you want there. What we need to settle first is the layout that's going to make this reorganization work."

Here the interruption is abrupt and does not support what's being said. Demizio takes off from the speaker's point and moves in her own direction. (Medical doctors seem addicted to this strategy, jumping into the middle of a patient's story of pain or problem with "Ever get ringing in your ears?" or "Was your mother left-handed?") West and Zimmerman call this tactic a way of "doing" power in face-to-face interactions. Language from the Center, as a directive speech style, uses interruption to manage the conversation and to maintain an agenda.

The directive speaker may do power and claim turf by "parking" in a conversation, as well. Expressions or utterances that allow a speaker to step into a conversation and then "play for time," organizing thoughts while also holding the floor, are bids for control. "Uhhhh" and "Well" do the job. Holding the floor is also possible with a string of "and's." Children's speech exemplifies this strategy. Kids literally keep Mom or Dad from getting a word in edgewise: "I was on the way to school and I saw Jamie up the block and she had this funny-looking suitcase with her and I could see it was sort of heavy and I wanted to see what was in it and she was way ahead of me and . . ." All grown up, this speaker may jump in with an empty phrase like "That being said . . . ," take over the conversation before she offers a real idea, and maintain her spot with a similar string of "and's." John Dean, during the Watergate hearings, invented the place holder "At this point in time." He seemed to be answering the question, but was actually composing his answer. Expressions like "all things being equal" or "that being said" have no substantive meaning in conversation. These lead-off phrases (Goffman calls them "weak bridges") add little to the topic at hand except as an acknowledgment of the need for continuity. No one talks about all things being unequal—what all things?—or ever presents a thought founded on "that not being said." Like "To be frank" or "Well, to be perfectly honest," these expressions are formalized pauses or transitions that allow a speaker to stake a claim in the conversation and head in his or her own direction.

With Language from the Center, then, this speaker directs the conversation, sets the true agenda, initiates topics and timing, and is able to redirect or recapture control of the conversation. Since every conversation is a bit of a turf war where several speakers want to establish the agenda, Demizio's Language from the Center keeps her life efficient, makes the most of the twenty-four hours in her day, and keeps both her internal and external clients on track.

2. MAKES STATEMENTS

Several years ago, a group of colleagues organized a petition to the school administration and then began urging the rest of the faculty to sign it. Some were eager to do so. I wasn't sure I endorsed this method of communicating with the administration.

But I was sure I didn't want to alienate my department colleagues. Then I overheard a fellow teacher deal with the issue. "I don't sign petitions," she said with an indulgent smile, almost as if the petitioners really ought to have known her policy on the matter. Her statement ended their plea and seemed to place her decision in a long-standing and well-thought-out philosophical context. It struck me at the time as a bold strategy.

Language from the Center favors statements. The speaker is confident and presents information by declaration:

"We need to consider the whole space."
"I'm sure we can meet the budget and still give you what you want."
"You'll like the way I've put this together."

The speaker is the presenter. The listener is the audience. Ideas are delivered by one to the other in a direct and forceful manner.

Likewise, if the listener raises questions or concerns, the speaker offers solutions or advice. The tone of the conversation is not exploratory; it is informational. This speech style is characterized by its "instrumentality": speech is used to solve problems, discover facts, and offer solutions. The listeners are students learning from the master, rather than a team collaborating on the matter in hand. Deborah Tannen, in her book *You Just Don't Understand*, looks at the sociolinguistics of gender and concludes that men are more likely to speak with instrumentality. Tannen calls it "report talk," talking to exhibit knowledge. In Demizio's case, the same rubric but clearly not the same gender issue applies. She needs to grab the spotlight, hold the floor, and speak to the group about the project and her product.

For Demizio, instrumentality is also the logical result of her expertise. She has been in the field for eleven years and knows her product. She can anticipate a substantial percentage of the problems, issues, and back-end snarls that are going to characterize a project. When her clients ask about flexibility, she has a ready answer about modular cubes. When they wonder what will make support staff happy, she has a study of ergonomics to share. Because clients tend to leave the furniture decision to the last minute, Demizio needs to move things along quickly, no matter how unsophisticated her clients are at the start of the process. By telling her clients as much as she can about product options and specifications, she hopes to close the deal. To be paid well, to generate a steady flow of business, she needs to focus on "Done."

Demizio's language choices are shaped by her situation. She delivers a lot of information in every conversation. It is her situation, however, rather than her gender, that determines her speech style. Any situation where expertise and knowledge is important will encourage this element of Language from the Center: the style of statements.

3. CONTEXTUALIZES WITH AUTHORITY

When Demizio first talked to Mike Scheff, she knew something about their operation from the previous job but not much about what they wanted to accomplish this time. Scheff explained the motive behind the reorganization. Both management and the associates wanted an environment that would allow them to interact spontaneously and efficiently: "They need a setting where they can exchange ideas on the spot and don't have to hunt down a meeting room somewhere. Jack [the CEO] wants contact to happen when and where it needs to happen," Scheff explained.

With the team-building research from one of her vendors and a quick review of previous projects like this one, Demizio sets out to convey her qualifications for this job. A battery of industry buzzwords can suggest credibility and the aura of experience. Knowing what to call things (like Adrienne's file puppy) is already part of Demizio's vocabulary of expertise. Long ago, she mastered the terminology of her work, the slang expressions and acronyms that streamline talk around the office. She knows the lore of the business as well as the lingo: the great projects, the legendary sales people, the worst mistake ever made. As a veteran, Demizio builds power from all this and more, mixing the legends and buzzwords into a context of authority. During her presentation, she makes connections to her expertise and previous experience:

"When we did this for Fidelity . . ."
"This is something I've done for several other clients . . ."
"When Alliance came to us for this kind of setup . . ."

Language from the Center uses authority and experience as a base. Numerous studies show that people accept leadership from those they perceive to be experts. Contextualizing a statement with a source of knowledge or authority adds substantial legitimacy. A bald list of your achievements and past clients belongs on a resume or on promotional material, but indirect references to credentials, authorities, research, numbers, or past projects establishes expertise:

"You know Al Johnson . . . we did their whole layout."
"We've got a history in the industry—my first project was to accommodate new word-processing equipment for a big publishing house back in the seventies. I've done every kind of tech interface there is."
"I've looked at your annual reports for the last five years and I think I see an interesting pattern that may impact this decision."

Demizio also uses another effective strategy for claiming authority—the analogy:

Project manager: "This seems like a good plan but I'm wondering, what if the team thing bombs and we have to go back to the departments we've always had?"
Demizio: "Remember when FirstCo joined information systems with their research department? It seemed like

a great idea and OC did the reengineering for them. One year later: divorce. But with modular units like the ones I've spec'd for you, they were able to make the adjustment with only installation expenses."

Here, Demizio connects the present situation to a parallel situation from the past. In pointing to an analogous job, she resolves her client's doubts.

Her analogy also suggests previous experience and knowledge thorough enough to allow for comparison. "That's the same problem we faced with AT&T" shows that she's covered this ground before, is familiar with the territory, and not worried about the outcome. Lawyers do this when they conjure up hundreds of pages of testimony and the details of a complicated controversy just by saying *Plessy v. Ferguson* or *Dennis v. New York*. Demizio conjures up past projects in the same way, by noting a parallel in the present situation to a situation she's already handled. The analogy helps Demizio avoid any negative judgment that might be made where speakers, especially women, showcase their own accomplishments. Analogies circumvent boasting about past triumphs but still claim authority with a shorthand for experience.

Facts—numbers, statistics, reports—give support to a claim of authority, as well. As in any argument, evidence builds position:

> "Studies have shown lighting can increase productivity as much as 25 percent."
> "You can figure on an eight- to ten-year life cycle for this kind of a setup."

A single, surprising fact, an unexpected piece of critical or new information, can be especially persuasive. In fact, an idea that is the opposite of what everyone else is thinking can win the day. Remember the kid in literature class who said, "Actually, the way I read it, *King Lear* is a comedy." She's a six-figure consultant now who wins clients with "Actually your problem isn't marketing at all. It's morale." So Demizio can grab control and claim authority with a surprise: "We find most clients use only about 10 percent of their files."

Significant specialization can also put you at the center of a conversation. The new hire with Web-site-creation experience, the colleague who specializes in start-up companies, the board member who's a professional writer, are heard on related topics because of their significant specialization. Bold assertion and specific references suggest a body of expertise, the tip of a knowledge iceberg that establishes Demizio as someone who's been around, done the research, and can be trusted by her clients.

Contextualizing with authority brings knowledge and experience into the conversation and, with it, credibility. But credibility is hard to maintain if there's a sense of personal involvement. Authority must be based on real information, not on personal assertions ("Trust me on this" or "I'm really excited about this project"). A renowned international negotiations expert explains his successful strategy: "I make it very clear that I care . . . but not too much." Experts avoid personal issues as much as possible and do not empathize or trade "me too" stories with the listener. Demizio talks about trade shows, space studies, and past projects rather than her brother-in-law's office or how much she loves the color blue. Her plan is offered within a framework of her information, objectivity, and experience: these credentials give her the "right" to be heard. Neutrality supports authority. The more Demizio seems like a consultant to NEB in working out the details of the project, the more credible she will seem. The more they think about her commission-based salary, the less credible she will seem.

Surprisingly, authority can also be established by humor. The speaker who can make light of a topic demonstrates comfort in the circumstances and familiarity with the issues. The humor of the stand-up comic or the joke-of-the-week belong on late-night TV. But researchers like Robert R. Provine, a professor of neurobiology and psychology at the University of Maryland, Baltimore County, who study laughter and humor in common conversation, see laughter as "social glue," rather than a response to something inherently funny. Laughter binds speaker and listener. Most of the time, no one is telling jokes. But within the course of a conversation, tension is reduced and connections are made with humor. This is why when the boss laughs, everybody laughs. So Demizio makes her client comfortable with occasional good-natured humor:

> Project manager: "We need to consider the possibility of another acquisition and therefore an expansion of this department."
>
> Demizio: "Well, as I see it, this layout would let you add up to ten more stations without moving the department to a different floor."
>
> Project manager: "I'm wondering though, are we just shooting ourselves in the foot here if we don't consider a what-if scenario . . . a really big explosion in the business."
>
> Demizio: "What factors might lead to that kind of expansion?"
>
> Project manager: "Hmmmmm, I don't know, I'm just speculating, I can't really see it but . . ."
>
> Demizio: "Sounds like your foot is safe to me."

Any speaker, boss or new hire, can use context-related humor to suggest comfort, connection, and the ease of authority. Just don't confuse contextual humor with forwarding jokes from an e-mail list, the electronic equivalent of playing with dynamite.

Each group, meeting, or audience represents a specific speech situation or context. What sounds like authority doesn't change, but the mix may. Facts and statistics can work well where financial concerns are primary. Analogies and references to previous projects can calm fears in start-up meetings. (You can often claim the high ground in a faculty meeting by speaking of "the life of the mind.") Choosing the right mix of expertise is part of the challenge. Outright self-congratulation and long litanies of achievement usually backfire. Such direct displays of excellence create resentment; studies have shown that such displays, particularly by women, can provoke negative responses. And claims of expertise that diminish others in a group are most unwelcome. Expect that some listeners will be resistant to your claims. Every meeting is, after all, a turf war. The situation is never simple, but if you are looking for power, then authority and expertise can help.

4. CONTRADICTS, ARGUES, AND DISAGREES

Language from the Center includes conflict. The speaker will contradict (as we saw in the pattern of interruption) or disagree with another speaker. She isn't angry or emotional, nor is she attacking the other person directly. But she has a different idea, one she views as more complete or more accurate than the one she's listening to. She may buttress this with a claim of authority or marshal the standard weapons of formal argument: objectivity, factual evidence, subversion of the counterargument. She will stick to her point and try to persuade the audience of its correctness. Again, because Language from the Center is directive and tends to view the audience as there to learn, this speaker will be bold about her idea and committed to its correctness. Her script may be "You're wrong about that," or a more conditional "I would argue that." Either way, she will return to her point during the conversation, recapitulate, and add more proof. With tenacity, evidence, and a confident presentation, she will try to undermine the opposition.

> "Yes, you're right, it's pretty to look at . . . but that's not the message you want to convey."
> "Remember though, their plan doesn't consider depreciation."
> "You need to figure in maintenance; it's not an expensive line if you look at the life-cycle cost."
> "The numbers over time don't bear that out."

Most important, Language from the Center argues through positive strengths, rather than through comparative strategies. Salary negotiations aren't focused on what Jones and Chen are being paid, but on the excellence of Demizio's work and her plans for next year. The best reason for NEB to choose the Primo Line isn't because other banks are remodeling with it but because the Primo Line will enhance the department's productivity. Language from the Center argues by looking forward not by looking around.

Language from the Center takes on risk for the sake of an idea and declares opinion boldly. It isn't abrasive nor is it personal. The speaker values the "correct" view over polite compliance and is willing to tolerate disagreement and even disagreeable responses for the sake of her own point of view.

5. PRACTICES AFFECT OF CONTROL

Chris Slaughter, an Army Ranger and a member of the Explosive Ordnance Disposal (EOD), knows the business of defusing bombs. Sometimes he unpacks a ticking box of nothing. Sometimes he is called in to take apart a detonator, a clock, and enough dynamite to sink Manhattan. In his off-hours, Slaughter tends bar in the Indiantown Gap officers' club. Since the bars in adjacent Harrisburg, Pennsylvania, close down at 2 A.M. and the officers' club stays open until 4 A.M., Slaughter sees more than his share of people at the end of an evening. Once in a while it falls to him to explain to a patron that the bar can no longer take responsibility for serving him or her additional alcoholic beverages. For Slaughter, the right way to handle this situation is with confidence, very few words, and dispatch. "I usually just jump the bar and jam the guy into the parking lot before he knows what hit him," says Slaughter. Does this ever cause trouble for Slaughter? Wouldn't it be more appropriate to inquire about the drinker's health, explore with him his present condition, and offer several supportive options for his journey home (taxi, friend, designated driver)?

"No, that doesn't work," says Slaughter. "People get very aggressive if you give them that kind of space. You've got to take the initiative, to act. It puts them on the defensive. They start accounting for themselves right away . . . 'Hey, wait a minute, I'm okay . . . really.' I've never run anybody out the door who didn't come back the next weekend, take me aside, and apologize." Slaughter's style works well on a military base (or a starship). The model for the affect of control is warriors who give unquestioning allegiance to their leaders who in turn appear brave, reliable, and wise. With a laser sword in your hand, you can say things like "You will bring Captain Solo and the Wookiee to me."

But what parts of the military model create the affect of control in traditional work? Confidence, brevity, and unemotional behavior are transferable skills. Michael Lewis in *Liar's Poker*, his account of the bond trader's life at Salomon Brothers in the 1980s, recalls: "It was stinking how little control we had of events, particularly in view of how assiduously we cultivated the appearance of being in charge." Sometimes, if the market's going to tank, the best thing to do is to shut up. Think of an athlete who has just lost a key point, game, hole on the golf course, or race at the swim meet. He can look beaten, mumble angry statements to himself, and slam his racquet, club, or towel on the ground. But this is not the affect of control. If he can stand up straight, look at those around him, keep his unhappy comments to himself and his facial expressions under control, he is in much better shape to succeed. Demizio has researched her presentation, talked to a number of people, pulled papers and floor plans from all her file drawers, and still plans to walk through the door at New England Bank like she owned the place. To support Language from the Center, she will need both the speech conventions and the matching body language of control.

Virginia Valian, in *Why So Slow?*, her encyclopedic review of the research on work and gender, suggests that impersonality, in particular, allows listeners to focus on your ideas rather than on distractions about you as a person; reserve and respect can act as a complement to competence and achievement. Valian notes, "An impersonal but friendly speaking style that conveys respect for others' opinions can help a professional . . . be perceived as a leader." Eye contact, minimal facial response, good posture, a moderate tone of voice, and an unemotional presentation add to the aura of assurance.

Interestingly, the affect of confidence appears to enhance performance. Acting like you know what you're doing can contribute to success. Studies among both students and athletes suggest that confidence about a performance improves the likelihood of success. Medical studies have demonstrated an improved survival rate for cancer patients who set out to "lick the big C" (compared with those who resign themselves to their illness). You can capitalize on the connection between attitude and outcome.

The United States Tennis Association hires umpires who know how to use the affect of control on the job. Training to call lines for a tennis match involves mastery of the rules of tennis (there are only forty). You need to train your eye and practice three hand signals. But the actual language of the job is simple: "Out" and "Fault" are all that's required. What makes a great line judge or chair umpire, besides good eyes and a commitment to fairness, is the confidence and economy of the call. Trainers tell new umpires to "Sell the call." The tone of voice, volume, facial expression, posture, and carefully timed call and hand signals are all meant to reinforce the validity of the single-word decision. Selling the call is Language from the Center, an essential style where judgment is required, whether by competing athletes or by company presidents. Concise and simply worded responses coupled with the unemotional and confident body language of Language from the Center can "sell the call" on an out ball or a question about desk heights.

Finally, the affect of control is useful when you haven't a clue as to what's going on but want to look like you do. As the Book of Proverbs tells us, "Even a fool, when he holds his peace, is counted wise." Sociologist Jack Sattel's insightful essay on inexpressiveness explores the power implicit in saying nothing. Sattel sees silence as a way "to consolidate power, to make the effort appear as effortless, to guard against showing the real limits of one's potential and power." Silence cannot create power but it can guard a powerful position. Marlon Brando provides a memorable example in *The Godfather*.

SUMMARY

Does leadership come with a job title? Do powerful people sound important because they are judges and managers and CEO's? Job, salary, uniform, title, or a spacious office can set the stage for power. But language style is another public power marker. When a manager calls together a committee, meets with a department, or confers with the company president, she

chooses words and a style of expression that confirm her position. An aspiring manager might choose Language from the Center when she is not the biggest title in the room, if she wants to claim more authority. She may be one of twenty new hires in the training class and yet decide, consciously, to establish credibility in the discussion. Since we accept the power of those who are experts, a confident affect and the language of leadership can begin to establish expertise.

Herminia Ibarra, a professor at the Harvard Business School, studied young investment bankers after their first promotion. Ibarra found that junior people consciously worked on the appearance of competence. One subject reported, "I had a fear of talking to clients, that they knew I didn't know anything. I still don't know but I'm learning to hide it." Another subject commented: "Style's another word for intelligence."

All the elements of the situation we find ourselves in affect word choice, syntax, inflection, and body language. With increased consciousness of the impact of these choices, however, we can make different—sometimes better—choices. Taken together, the elements of Language from the Center set the direction for the conversation and claim the right to do so. Language from the Center sounds like authority. Like any claim of power, it can inspire jealousy, resentment, and competition. Used wisely, it inspires confidence, trust, and respect.

THE PRICE OF LANGUAGE FROM THE CENTER

You may not feel that Language from the Center is the right tool for your job. But different jobs require different tools. And as work and status progress, Language from the Center becomes increasingly important. You can't move up and move on without authority. Cynthia Danaher, of Hewlett-Packard's Medical Products Group in Andover, Massachusetts, made the transition to general manager with a hefty challenge: running a small division of a large corporation (and getting some attention for it). She learned to pitch her expertise, to set direction, to delegate, and to claim her authority. But to do this, she had to learn "a new language." The style that made her a success at the entry and mid-levels undercut her authority in her new job and made her too available. "I felt a lot of grief letting go of who I'd been," Danaher told *Wall Street Journal* reporter Carol Hymowitz.

Language from the Edge and the inclusion it employs convey approachability and friendliness. Language from the Center and the power it conveys sets a speaker apart. It is often the primary speech style of doctors, judges, and police officers, and rarely the first choice of librarians, teachers, counselors, or therapists. Where there is authority, there is sometimes resentment and usually singularity, perhaps unwelcome isolation. The speaker bent on establishing credibility, neutrality, and distance doesn't leave much room for other voices. Former Drexel Burnham junk bond king Michael Milken was apparently notorious for this style. According to a former colleague, "Mike's difficulty was that he simply didn't have the patience to listen to another point of view. . . . If Mike hadn't gone into the securities business, he would have led a religious revival movement." Language from the Center establishes the power of leadership, but the lead dog doesn't run with the pack.

TROUBLE IN PARADISE

For Demizio, sales and Language from the Center are a natural match since sales requires the aura of authority associated with Language from the Center. So is Demizio the perfect sales rep? Her revenues suggest she is. She gets the job done and brings in the business. Her clients are loyal and she's been with OC long enough now that many of them are repeat orders. Still, her boss isn't happy.

Demizio's boss explains:

> I can never get her to listen. She's like a fountain of facts. I feel like she's all over every meeting we have and the client never gets to talk about the problems,

the vision of the company, the unusual constraints. Then the whole thing craters because there was this big, important thing we didn't know.

She doesn't know how to ask questions. She only knows how to unload. She's all about product, even to the management-level deciders who don't want to know about divider heights. And they only give you so many chances. She does a great job with answers. But sometimes she hasn't bothered to figure out what the questions are. When you don't know the end-user, things fall apart.

Her team feels pushed around, too. Her project manager feels bullied. The design people feel like she can't be bothered with them—she wants her stuff now and that's all she cares about. We're concerned about her ability to work with her team . . . and we don't like the number of projects that blow up at the last minute because of key information we needed to know—and didn't know—when the job was spec'd.

Demizio is terrific when she's working from the center. But she has only one approach to every problem: take control and tell them what they ought to know. While this is great in the educational part of her work, the initial stages of her work with clients and the collaborative meetings with her design team need a different language. Everybody loves Demizio's productivity, but they feel like she never shuts up. She needs flexibility of style and a little cross-training in Language from the Edge.

CHAPTER TWO
LANGUAGE FROM THE EDGE

"Timid is how deer stay alive."
JACK ELDER, editor of Citibank *Economic Week*

Tom Hanks turns his head slightly to the right and peers into the darkness. His spacecraft is spiraling out of control, white vapor streaming from its flank. "Houston, we have a problem." In the film *Apollo 13*, Hanks portrays NASA astronaut James A. Lovell Jr., commander of an ill-fated spacecraft. His understated communication of the ship's loss of both oxygen and orbit path is what Language from the Center sounds like. As the commander, he is directive, declarative, and full of authority. He ought to be—he's the one spiraling toward the edge of the universe.

But speakers aren't always at the center. Sometimes, it's not an option. You're unfamiliar with the topic or new to the position, you're not involved in the issue under consideration, or someone else has taken over. Or you may be experienced, knowledgeable, and involved and yet choose to move out of the center, to let others direct the conversation or take control.

What if Hanks had radioed this message: "Houston, I'm probably not the best judge of this but I'm just wondering . . .

do you think we might have a problem?" The general content hasn't changed—the speaker is still concerned about a new difficulty—but the construction of this message conveys a different sense of the speaker. He is not at the center of the situation; he's on the edge. The use of a question rather than a statement, the disclaimer that precedes it, the auxiliary "might" to establish contingency, all conspire to place the speaker out of the center of power. He raises a concern, defers to wiser heads than his own, and leaves it to Houston to sort things out.

Specific speech conventions indicate when a speaker is not in the driver's seat, not the commander of the flight. Language from the Edge, like Language from the Center, has its own parameters, its own features and identifying characteristics. And it creates a balance of power quite different from Language from the Center.

WHAT LANGUAGE FROM THE EDGE SOUNDS LIKE

1. Responds Rather Than Directs
2. Asks Questions
3. Contextualizes with Protective Strategies
4. Avoids Open Argument
5. Practices Conversational Maintenance

WHAT LANGUAGE FROM THE EDGE CONVEYS

Language from the Center is directive and authoritative. Language from the Edge, on the other hand, is careful, exploratory, and inquiring. It is inclusive, deferential, and collaborative. The speaker asks questions, reacts responsively, and practices conversational maintenance. He is exploring the topic at hand: listening, learning, and gathering, rather than directing. He seems approachable, personable, interested in the other people in the conversation. He nods when others speak. He defers when he lacks information. He stops the conversation to ask for clarification or directs the conversation to another speaker. Language from the Edge is its own set of strategies but, like Language from the Center, it offers a predictable box of tools.

LANGUAGE FROM THE EDGE SOUNDS LIKE INQUIRY, APPROACHABILITY, INCLUSION

Andrew Godfrey sits down behind his desk and looks you straight in the eye. Shoulders squared, he inclines into the space between you. He is ready to listen. Godfrey is a lawyer with a division of an international hydrocarbon company headquartered in Geneva, Switzerland. With annual net income in the billions, Godfrey's company comprises exploration, production, refining, chemical production, and the manufacture of pharmaceutical, health, and beauty products. As a specialist in environmental law, Godfrey, along with the director of risk management and several other in-house counselors, reports to the senior vice president/general counsel of the chemical division headquartered in Lexington, Kentucky.

Godfrey's day is about meetings. With five other attorneys assigned to specific project responsibilities, he looks at a weekly calendar full of meetings with state and federal regulators like the EPA, with operating management from any one of the company's plants, and with attorneys from other firms looking to sort out complicated questions of responsibility and liability. A few white spaces on his day-planner get eaten up by contacts with his own department.

Not surprisingly, Godfrey's speech style is cautious. As an environmental lawyer, he's paid to keep the company out of trouble. That means every question needs to be asked twice. Back in 1985, the company acquired a subsidiary with an overlooked and complicated cleanup obligation. The problems are still being sorted out in the courts of Texas. "Once burned, twice shy" means Godfrey's department had better not get it wrong a second time.

Godfrey's overall conversational style is Language from the Edge. At meetings that bring together teams of engineers, chemists, plant operations personnel, and subcontractors, Godfrey does not set the agenda or direct the conversation. He asks for clarifications and fields the legal questions. Plant managers talk process, engineers talk design and implementation, the CFO is there to be sure the bottom line is in view; Godfrey's role is to point out problems, keep an eye on compliance, and make sure nothing slips by.

Godfrey is on the edge, but not entirely by choice; his job as counsel puts him there. And his news is often bad news; his contributions to the conversation slow things down, raise red flags, and lead to increased costs. Godfrey's training as a lawyer might seem likely to produce a speaker ready to take charge, but in fact, his work and his company context encourage Language from the Edge.

1. RESPONDS RATHER THAN DIRECTS

When the plant manager from the Tyler, Texas, acrylics processing site came to Lexington to meet with engineers about a new line of paint bases, Godfrey was at the meeting. The majority of the conversation focused on production rates: costs, quality, and transportation. But emissions, waste handling, and disposal all involved Godfrey's input. Godfrey responds rather than directs in most of the meetings he attends and he didn't control the direction of this meeting, either. He dropped into the conversation when his area of expertise—federal and state air and water pollution regulations—was relevant.

CFO: "I need to see some comparable figures from our
other plants."
Tyler plant manager: "We can count on returns similar to
those at Paducah, Springfield, and Tulsa."
Godfrey: "I'm wondering though . . . I don't think—what
with all the restrictions on this kind of material—are
any of these figures really going to be comparable?"

Edge speakers don't set the agenda. They respond to what's
already out there. They join in when their area of expertise is
the topic, but they rarely affect the primary direction of the
conversation. They work from the perimeter, shaping and
prodding with small contributions. If they make definitive
statements, they are usually responding to questions directed
to them. Like border collies trained to manage sheep, they
may keep the flock drifting toward the barn, but they don't
lead the way.

Even when Godfrey runs a meeting, he often employs Language from the Edge. Bringing his department together to
brainstorm their computing needs, Godfrey does very little
talking and a lot of listening. He drops into the "wish list"
frenzy, asks questions, and lets the conversation take its own
direction. He yields to other speakers who feel the homegrown
software works best. He invites those who want to standardize
the programs to pitch their point of view. He asks questions
about Flaherty's request for Westlaw and Ng's preference for
Lexus. He tries to be sure everyone is heard:

Godfrey: "It sounds like we're pretty happy with what
we've got . . . but now, Jen [he laughs], I know you feel
like it's only a matter of time before we're going to have
to change. That's right, isn't it?"

Where teams collaborate on a shared project, the project
leader may choose this inclusive and exploratory style. But
working from the edge remains a responsive rather than a directive style.

2. ASKS QUESTIONS

Questions are essential to Language from the Edge.

> Godfrey: "I'm wondering though . . . I don't think—what with all the restrictions on this kind of material—are any of these figures really going to be comparable?"

Godfrey drops in to raise an objection. He doesn't like using one product to predict outcomes for another. But he phrases his objection as a question—"are any of these figures really going to be comparable?"—rather than as a statement: "You can't predict production in a new product by looking at an existing product." As part of the general counsel staff, he is a consultant in the Tyler plant meeting and he asks about what others propose. With his own group, he asks for confirmation of a point from Jen, the dissenter. Asking questions is how speakers on the edge get involved.

Godfrey chooses a question to highlight his reservations about predictions. He works from the edge because questions, in and of themselves, ask for help. They defer power to the other party as a source of knowledge. Our schooling has conditioned us to see questions this way. And we judge the inquirer for making the inquiry. You've probably been in a meeting or signed up for training and found yourself next to the guy with a million questions. It wasn't long before the whole class was making eye contact and looking heavenward every time his hand went up. "I was just wondering . . ." The teacher may have had patience for the eighth or ninth question, but the class grew increasingly frustrated and intolerant. By the end of the hour, you were edging your chair as far away as possible, fully convinced that the negative aura of this helpless guy might rub off on you.

Even small children make judgments about help. A study of elementary school children established a clear judgment between two students, one whose work elicited a helping comment from the teacher and one whose work did not. The children watched a videotape of two boys taking a math test. Their teacher circulated and looked at both boys' papers. To one boy she said, "Don't forget to carry your tens." To the other boy, she said nothing. The children watching the videotape were told that both boys did equally well on their assignment. But the children were then asked which boy they would like as a future math partner. Most chose the boy who had not been helped. The need for assistance influences our judgment about a speaker's knowledge and competence. The questions associated with Language from the Edge sound like requests for help.

The linguist and author Deborah Tannen, in *You Just Don't Understand,* considers a specific request for help: asking for directions. Tannen concludes that the stereotypical male does not ask for directions. She recounts several vivid anecdotes of men who drove in circles for hours rather than pull over to ask for help. The stereotype surfaces in a popular joke: "Why did the tribes wander for forty years in the desert? Because Moses wouldn't ask for directions." But questions in an area where you are supposed to be knowledgeable are the most damaging. We can't assume that, had Judith taken over leadership of the tribes, a good road map would have materialized. Any leader is going to feel that asking for directions compromises position. If the men in Tannen's research didn't ask, it may have been because they felt it was their responsibility to know. Viewing themselves as in charge, with the power balance on their side, they may not have wanted to open the power arrangement to question (literally). Those who want to appear at the center don't use questions. And while Tannen associates the reluctance to ask for directions with men (and the willingness to seek help with women), she acknowledges the whole transaction is, at its heart, "a move in the negotiation of status." Power is the influential element. Thus, for both men and women, asking for directions if you're supposed to know where you are is an admission of ignorance. And we're conditioned to believe that questions aren't where the power resides.

Not every question, however, is an admission of ignorance. Godfrey, for example, is asking questions in order to clarify and highlight information he mostly understands. Still, questions by nature are deferential. Michael Lewis's *Liar's Poker* describes a question strategy that surfaced in his first few months at Salomon Brothers:

> A hand shot up (typically) in the front row . . . "I was just wondering," said Findlay, "if you could tell us what you think has been the key to your success." This was too much. . . . The back row broke out in its loudest laughter yet. Someone cruelly mimed Findlay in a high-pitched voice. "Yes, *do* tell us why you're *sooooo* successful."

Lewis's training class was intensely competitive. After all, the company's chairman required every trader to wake each morning "ready to bite the ass off a bear." In such an environment (like any school class), this question's deference revealed it to be blatant brownnosing. Power is in answers. In a highly competitive setting, be careful what you ask.

Questions can dress up like statements and still be questions. Every Thanksgiving my dad asked my mom, "When's dinner?" She responded, "At four?" To choreograph the meal around the vagaries of football games—games that might last as long as thirty minutes after the two-minute warning had been given—she offered her plans for approval by Dad and the Detroit Lions. She stated the time with the rising inflection of a question. So while the meal ought to have been at the discretion of the cook, Mom chose Language from the Edge on this one, rather than see the food get cold while somebody went for the extra point.

Like other questions, inflected questions convey a tentative and inquiring tone. This is the tone of every "Hello" we say into the phone. It may be the tone of your answer when the boss says, "I need this back by five." You say, "You need this back *by five*?" However, the inflected question can be a dangerous speech habit, an unconscious sound sequence that cushions your statements and turns your declarations into questions. You think you're making statements. But when you sound like you're "asking" a statement and seeking confirmation, you are working from the edge.

> "I'm the new temp? I started on Monday? Can you show
> me where they keep the toner cartridges?"

That's three questions, not one.

The tag question is another deferential expression that converts a statement to a question. A tentative and invitational syntax, the tag question seeks a response from the listener.

> "The balance sheet is a problem, *isn't it?*"
> "He's sort of a control-freak, *isn't he?*"

The last phrase, the tag, seeks confirmation or collaboration. The speaker invites the listener into the conversation (probably why parents speaking to little children so consistently use this formula):

> "We've got all the things we need, *don't we?*"
> "The big dog scared you, *didn't he?*"

The same strategy underlies the added "okay": "I need this by five, *okay?* And it's got to be perfect, *okay?* Get everybody to sign off on it, *okay?*"

These inclusion tags are often unconscious speaking habits and they undercut the instrumentality of a statement. If you're working from the edge, they make sense as a way to temper your declaration. If you mean to adopt the directive style of Language from the Center, they are a mistake—and don't sound anything like: "I need this by five. It's got to be perfect. And everybody needs to sign off on it, too."

Questions are basic tools for Language from the Edge and they are useful for gathering information and involving other speakers. They effectively pass the ball. They're great when they're what you mean to say. But with all the baggage of judgment they bring, they need to be used with conscious intent.

QUESTIONS THAT DON'T ASK FOR HELP

Questions come in lots of flavors. Even though the classroom is where you learned to ask questions, it is also where you learned that questions can be a trap. Teachers themselves ask a lot of questions: "When did Columbus discover America? What's the capital of Nebraska? Who was poet laureate of England in 1850?" To these questions, they already have the answers . . . and they have a sneaking suspicion you don't.

Questions designed to embarrass or discredit the person to whom they are addressed represent an effort to seize power. These "challenge questions" are not asked for the purpose of gathering information; these are the "teacher questions," the ones to which the asker already knows the answer. They are asked to establish the asker's expertise.

Consider this scenario. Albatross.com's representatives show up to make a presentation to potential investors that includes an overview of a company's financial prospects. The investors are wary, but they're listening. When the cash flow slide hits the screen, Rachel notices a computational error: "Isn't capital spending usually *deducted* from cash flow?" The question is rhetorical. Rachel knows she's caught a mistake and, like your sixth-grade teacher, she just threw a pop quiz at Albatross.com's people. They're on the spot, making the pitch and hoping to impress the investors. The investors are in control so Rachel can swagger a little here because she knows she's right (and she just feels like putting these guys' feet to the fire). Since most conversations—and all meetings—are turf wars, these kinds of questions are power plays and are not really part of the inquiry or collaboration of Language from the Edge.

The same holds true for "question/answers." The conventions of conversation dictate that questions should receive answers. When questions prompt questions in response, the standard back-and-forth of the conversation is broken. This may be done, as Godfrey did, in order to facilitate the conversation:

"What numbers do we need for this report?"
"Do we know who's going to be reading it?"

But as a power play, it can be done to avoid the question and to shift the role of respondent back onto the questioner.

Q: "What's your motivation in pursuing this project?"
A: "What do you mean by motivation?"

Even a tag question can claim the high ground. Linguist John Algeo, in his essay "It's a Myth, Innit?" shows how, especially in Britain, tag questions challenge the respondent and aggressively assert the speaker's point of view.

Wife: Haven't you started [papering the walls] yet?
Husband: Yeah, well pet, it's all preparation, *innit?*

Or in this example:

A: You need to go to your local police.
Q: I've done all that, *haven't I?*

Responsive questioning buys time and scrambles the speech conventions operating in a specific conversation. The respondent refuses his or her role and reassigns it to the questioner. Again, because this kind of question asserts rather than defers, it isn't Language from the Edge.

Godfrey doesn't use questions to capture power or embarrass management. Instead, he spends most of the morning sitting patiently at that marble slab in the chairman's office, listening and waiting. He asks questions in order to understand what liabilities might arise from this project. He asks about processes, costs, and disposal plans as a way of informing himself and as an indirect way of heightening others' awareness of these issues. His concerns and caveats sound like this:

"Have we checked this out with the local people?"
"We do have a full-time compliance officer on this site, don't we?"
"Has Geneva seen these drawings?"

He may return to his own department with fire in his eye and demand follow-ups from five different people who didn't prepare the right documents for this meeting, but in the conference room, he does his job best with the questions of Language from the Edge.

3. CONTEXTUALIZES WITH PROTECTIVE STRATEGIES

In Barry Sonnenfeld's 1997 film *Men in Black,* Will Smith plays a New York City cop recruited for a special assignment. Smith knows nothing about the job when he shows up for the interview and he finds himself in a vaultlike edifice with no clue as to what's going on. He walks into a room full of uniformed candidates who are intently listening to a presentation. He is greeted with, "You're late . . . sit down." Finally, he ventures to raise his hand: "Uh yeah, um um I'm sorry . . . ahhhh . . . maybe you already answered this. But . . . um . . . why exactly are we here?" Nothing has made the situation clear and Smith is forced to ask. He presents his question with an apology and a disclaimer: "Sorry . . . maybe you already answered this. . . ." Smith takes heat for the question and is silenced by the withering glances of the other candidates.

A speaker on the edge packages statements (even a question) with verbal bubble-wrap—a protective covering around the comment. Sometimes it's a disclaimer: "I know this may seem like a random question, but . . ." (Hence, the posters in many a classroom designed to counter question anxiety: "There's no such thing as a stupid question.")

"I know this is beside the point . . ."
"This may not be relevant . . ."
"You've probably already covered this . . ."

It may be an apology:

"I'm sorry, but . . ."
"I hate to mention cost . . ."

Or a personalization of the comment:

"This is probably just my problem . . ."
"I guess I'm being paranoid here but . . ."

Even the simple insertion of the word "just" adds significant protective impact. This little adverb demotes the concern, thought, or effort and takes the power out of almost any verb:

"I'm just worried that . . ."
"I was just thinking . . ."
"I'm just the coordinator of this project."

(Try rereading these statements without the "just" and you'll hear the difference.)

Language from the Edge—responsive, questioning, and tentative—strives to soften the impact of a comment with verbal hedges. Just as the question "Do you think we might have a problem?" leaves more room to maneuver than the statement "We have a problem," the disclaimer, the apology, or the personalization lets the listener discount what follows. The strategy offers a self-canceling context. Notice Godfrey, in his comment to the Tyler, Texas, people, begins by saying, "I'm wondering though . . ." The "I" in Godfrey's question makes the point purely personal. He's ready to admit this may not be everybody's first concern. Thus, when he says he's "just wondering . . . ," his point seems like a transitory thought, hardly worth mentioning.

4. AVOIDS OPEN ARGUMENT

As *Men in Black* progresses, Will Smith takes on "the best of the best" and he is ultimately chosen for the special assignment (he's the star, after all). By the film's climax, he can comfortably say to those who first doubted him, "Hey, old men!" But in those early scenes, out on the edge and away from the center of power, he can't challenge the men in charge. He can't even get them to call him by the right name. The speaker on the edge, then, is not likely to engage in open argument. She is responding, listening, adding information when appropriate, keeping things moving along. If she hears something problematic, she will ask a question. But she is unlikely to directly challenge another speaker.

Harvard Business School professor Herminia Ibarra, in her article "Deference and Demeanor: Gender, Demography and Self-Presentation in Professional Careers," describes the protective behaviors of mid-level investment bankers and management consultants and their unwillingness to challenge or argue. Although Ibarra found the style more common among the women than among the men she interviewed, both men and women in her study expressed a reserve that sounds like Language from the Edge: "I tend not to step out on a limb when I'm not fairly confident about an assertion. If I have an idea, I think to myself, 'Oh, that's stupid,' and I won't say it. . . . I think to myself, 'How can I tell this fifty-five-year-old guy who's been in the industry his whole life that his last investment was really stupid.'" Or "I don't feel comfortable saying something if I don't know what the answer is yet. I'm less comfortable challenging my clients when I don't know what they think."

In the same way, Godfrey may hear something from one of the plant managers that makes him nervous. Maybe a manufacturing process is being considered that Godfrey knows led to trouble before.

> "I'm wondering if this is going to lead to problems like we had with Waltec."
> "Have they worked out the bugs since '97?"

As legal adviser, he is not going to challenge openly or argue aggressively with any of the other participants in this meeting.

One result of the deference of Language from the Edge is the unfinished sentence. The speaker who habitually relies on this style may be interrupted by a speaker asserting power. If he is interrupted, he will yield the floor, letting others take over or join in.

> Godfrey: "Do we know why these filters aren't working? If we know what's causing the problems, then we can . . ."
> Andrea: "It's not about the filters. It's about measurement. There's nothing wrong with those stacks. We're just not getting consistent readings from the instruments."

Here Godfrey is interrupted by a speaker bent on changing the conversation's direction, using the interruption strategy described in Chapter 1. If Godfrey were working from the center, he would assert his power and interrupt back with "Hold on." But if he is working from the edge, he will defer and let his unfinished point pass. The unfinished sentence shows up not just because of an aggressive break-in but by intention. Some speakers even stop speaking before they are finished, in anticipation of interruption or as an invitation to another speaker to take over: "I don't know, I'm just wondering if the whole plan, the start-up costs, the timing, everything . . ."

As we saw in Chapter 1, most conversations are full of overlaps and interruptions—we even "interrupt" ourselves, changing course or content as our thoughts form. Some of these interruptions are the normal overlap of a fast-paced conversation. And some are affirmative interruptions of the "yeah, right" or "that's true" variety. Others are challenges to the speaker. But the speaker on the edge will defer to these other speakers rather than try to hold the floor; he will not contradict or interrupt others with a challenge and he often says only part of what he started to contribute.

5. PRACTICES CONVERSATIONAL MAINTENANCE

Language from the Edge cultivates the conversation. Nearly all the speech conventions described above keep the talk going, that is, they demonstrate conversational maintenance. The process is more important to this speaker than the turf. He isn't trying to lay down rules and give directions. Domination may not be possible or desirable at the moment; the energy of the talk is sufficient. Therefore, speakers on the edge ask other voices to join the conversation:

"Andrea, I need to know what you're thinking about this."

"What did marketing say about your idea?"

They build on what's just been said, creating a bridge from their own point to the ideas of others in the group. They acknowledge what has already been contributed to the discussion ("As Jen just said . . ."). They may reiterate, summarize, or elaborate on another speaker's comment:

"It sounds like what you're saying is . . ."
"Jen's concerned about two or five years out . . . am I right?"

They may address an individual within the group rather than direct their comments to the group as a whole, seeing the conversation as a group activity rather than as a presentation. Others in the group aren't necessarily the audience; they are part of the performance. The pattern of questioning, the responsive style, the deferential, inclusive, and contextualizing comments, the unfinished sentences, the connecting and collaborating all keep things going. Language from the Edge creates space into which other speakers move. It gathers rather than presents information. It is the speech of those who by position or by preference are put (or put themselves) outside the center of power, viewing personal authority as unavailable or less important than the power of ideas and talk.

SUMMARY

Language from the Center and the authority it claims conveys competence and control. Language from the Edge and the inclusion it employs conveys exploration and collaboration. Remember, however, this style conveys personal warmth and approachability. This is the consultant looking for input and ideas rather than the new CEO, full of declarations and decisions. It's the boss who's willing to listen, the team leader willing to share the power. Does it seem timid? Maybe. But when Jack Elder, editor of Citibank's newsletter, *Economic Week,* was accused of timidity in his forecasting, he quipped, "Timid is how deer stay alive."

The Price of Language from the Edge

You may not feel that Language from the Edge is the right tool for your job. It worked when you were a new hire and full of questions. It served you well at that company with the team philosophy. It may seem a style ill suited to a position of power. But it isn't only the proponents of Language from the Center who are listened to and promoted. It is possible to have authority and work from the edge. In work that depends on long-term relationships, in stable job settings with low turnover, in project-based work that assembles ad hoc teams requiring cross-department consensus, people succeed with very little Language from the Center. Jonathan Krakauer's Everest narrative *Into Thin Air* is a reminder of the risks that go with bold leadership: "Mountaineering tends to draw men and women not easily deflected from their goals. . . . Unfortunately, the sort of person who is programmed to ignore personal distress and keep pushing for the top is frequently programmed to disregard signs of grave and imminent danger as well." The price of nice may be the better bargain.

Perhaps one of the most successful managers who worked almost entirely with Language from the Edge was the legendary editor of *The New Yorker*, William Shawn. From 1952 until 1987, he guided the magazine and its writers in an unusually shy and formal way. Where a writer's word or expression was wrong, Shawn would note on the manuscript margin, "We avoid." Where an idea needed correction, he suggested that not he but rather "people who didn't really understand the magazine" objected. His employees found his style encouraging and inspiring. The power Shawn derived from his intelligence and commitment—rather than from his domination and demands—created loyalty, admiration, and affection in the writers he guided, chided, and corrected for thirty-five years. Shawn's power of long-term authority helped him lead from the edge. And Shawn's workers were an unusually sensitive crowd. (Brendan Gill writes that at times the writer's insecurity could drive him to wonder if his own signature couldn't stand

50

a little work!) Situation influences all speech choices, but situation can be shaped by both the power you hold and the power you give away.

TROUBLE IN PARADISE

For the most part, things run smoothly for Godfrey. He is available to his company when needed and knowledgeable on the issues of environmental law. His team feels they have input. His boss appreciates his caution. But last December Godfrey's performance review included:

> One developmental need relates to Andy's communication skills. In his oral communication, he needs to work on providing direct, succinct, to-the-point answers to questions, without background and extraneous information which often seems irrelevant and defensive. Increased directness in all areas would result in greater management confidence in Andy's role as a counselor/adviser. A lack of directness leads to the perception that Andy is unable to form an opinion and communicate it well, or that he is "playing politics." This undermines management's confidence in his overall contribution. Attention to the need for clarity of thought and direct expression can improve this problem.

Godfrey was shocked. How could he have a communication problem? He was a lawyer. Good communication skills were at the heart of his work. Words were his stock-in-trade. What was this all about? Godfrey's boss explained:

> This isn't about Andy's knowledge as a lawyer. The problem is Andy needs to give brief, clear answers that establish his authority with the management people. He seems hard to pin down, elusive. Like he

has this habit of letting a subordinate in his department answer important questions—he'll say "Seth and I discussed that last week, in fact, and . . ." Then he defers to Seth and lets him do the talking. I understand a natural caution—I'm a lawyer, too. But some of the internal people wonder if Andy knows enough. And the big guys wonder if he's being straight with them.

Working from the edge is generally a successful strategy for Godfrey. The problem is that he never uses any other style of speech. He is a collaborative and responsive listener but his department meetings go on for as long as anyone feels like talking. He knows his stuff but his style with internal clients isn't inspiring confidence. To people outside the department, he seems reactive and hesitant. Sometimes he seems bent on slowing things down or smothering every plan on the table with caveats and questions. As a lawyer, he is already perceived by many of the business managers as a potential source of delay. And his habit of Language from the Edge makes everyone a little paranoid: "What isn't he telling us? He's got a million questions. But geez, where do we stand?"

Like Demizio, in Chapter 1, Godfrey needs a little linguistic cross-training. His habitual speech style encourages his team and taps the energy and power of his colleagues' ideas. It helps him gather information and offer ideas in protected and deferential ways. But he isn't doing much to keep the managers, financial vice presidents, and the outside clients secure in his authority and expertise. Language from the Center will probably never be Godfrey's main mode of operation. Still, its strategies need to be in his toolbox.

CHAPTER THREE
LINGUISTIC
CROSS-TRAINING

Mrs. Pearce: . . . But you really must not swear in front of the girl.

Higgins [*indignantly*]: *I* swear! [*Most emphatically*] I never swear. I detest the habit. What the devil do you mean?

GEORGE BERNARD SHAW, *Pygmalion*

Nicholas Slonimsky, the encyclopedist and composer, published his life story, *Perfect Pitch,* at the end of a long and diverse career in the world of music. Every page is marked with the energy and passion he gave to more than eighty years of composing, conducting, and publishing. His recollections of his daughter, Electra's, birth and childhood are among the most endearing. Slonimsky was fascinated with his infant daughter, and as his wife was involved with work and he was between projects during Electra's preschool years, he spent an unusual amount of time with the child.

I began speaking Latin to her, inspired by a Polish couple, both professors of ancient languages in Warsaw who spoke to their offspring exclusively in Latin and Greek. I called Electra "Puella" and named household objects in Latin for her to learn.

Slonimsky recounts the progress of this experiment. Finally, however, Electra discovered a transforming truth: "One day Electra announced, with a suspicious look in her eyes, 'Daddy, other kids don't speak Latin at home.'"

Although Electra Slonimsky's experience seems unusual, it is, in fact, one shared by every child—we learn the language we hear. And we can talk our way through life largely unconscious of the differences, variations, or individual idiosyncrasies of our own speech. Thus, while Donna Demizio and Andrew Godfrey are successful professionals who bring both training and extensive experience to their respective jobs, they are not very knowledgeable about their own speech habits. Demizio is a top seller at her company and Godfrey has gotten to the assistant general counsel level. Still, both have the potential to be more successful if they can step back, listen to themselves, and do a little field research in their speech and in the world of words around them. The model for this process of observation is a four-step sequence useful to everyone who wants to practice linguistic cross-training and multiply options for successful communication.

THE FOUR STEPS OF LINGUISTIC CROSS-TRAINING

Looking In
Looking Out
Trying In
Trying Out

First, Demizio and Godfrey need to know something more about themselves. Their initial assignment is to study their own conversations. *Looking in* is the first challenge of linguistic cross-training. How do I sound in a meeting? In an interview? In a conversation? How much do I say? How long do I talk? How many questions do I ask? How confident do I sound? How much variety is there among the different con-versations in my day? Listening to—and thinking about—your own speech is difficult. But it is the first step in figuring out how speech adds to the impression you make and the power you claim.

Next, if they're interested in improving their options, De-mizio and Godfrey need to do some *looking out*. Every orga-nization has a speech culture or "register" of its own. The vocabulary and jargon of the field—investment advisers ver-sus computer salespeople versus florists' wholesalers—consti-tute the buzzwords of work, learned easily and almost unconsciously on the job. And where we want to assimilate, where joining a group is essential to succeeding, we quickly adopt the vocabulary of the group. "Looking out" means more than this, however. It involves determining the success-ful speech style and conventions of a particular office or work-place—what activist Jesse Jackson calls "the cash language." Do people offer ideas with tentative disclaimers or do they slap down bold declarations of how things need to be done? Do the powerful people direct their staff or prefer to work from the edge? Are rising stars rule-breakers or quiet respon-dents? Does management offer a model for the speech style most likely to succeed?

Looking out includes looking very closely at both the suc-cessful people and at the failures. It's exciting to observe the rainmakers and contemplate your own parallel path to power. But a look at those who aren't succeeding will tell you the most about what is prized and what is unwelcome in the world of your work.

The third step for Demizio and Godfrey (and for you) is ex-perimentation with the successful strategies. *Trying in* is a way of testing the feasibility of a new behavior or speech tactic. If you experiment in a small and friendly environment, you can gauge both your own comfort level and the response of others. These factors affect how likely you are to repeat and therefore incor-porate a strategy into your daily language repertoire. Trying in is the small-scale test-run that prepares you to make bigger changes.

Finally, *trying out* your new behavior involves using it in a more public setting. Knowing that you have options and choosing the right tool for the job can be empowering. While adding a more directive style of meeting management may not yield an immediate promotion, it can reassure your team and produce a welcome efficiency. Likewise, listening and working from the edge as a meeting organizer—saying "Go on" when a new idea is introduced, or "Give me an example" when a strategy is offered—can generate creativity, energy, and goodwill. It may uncover ideas or information of immediate value. An opponent, given enough rope, may even hang himself. And once in a while, someone else proposes the idea you thought would be a hard sell, and everyone climbs on board. Those are the good days.

But remember, language is closely tied to identity. Your speech is as individual as a fingerprint. Thus, awareness of your conversational style and access to new options won't override what is still going to be your core style. This four-step method won't remake you because you don't, in fact, need to be entirely remade. Remember Demizio still has that fat sales book. Godfrey has a solid record of keeping his company in compliance and out of trouble. But self-awareness and a conscious control of speech choices are two tools worth adding to the toolbox you've been using for years.

Let's look in detail at:

Looking In
Looking Out
Trying In
Trying Out

LOOKING IN

A LITTLE FIELDWORK

Speech research isn't easy. If you want to find out how people in Chicago pronounce the word "milk," you can grab a tape recorder and start asking passersby. But most respondents in such a situation offer what they think is the "right" pronunciation of the word—or even what they think you will think is the right pronunciation—not necessarily the pronunciation they use in normal conversation. And what exactly qualifies as a normal conversation? You could try having a bunch of dialogues in front of the supermarket dairy case—but that would be time-consuming and impractical.

These same challenges apply to the study of your own speech habits. What we say isn't easily captured and examined. We are very unreliable analysts of our own speech, unlikely to give unbiased or even accurate information. One study asked business executives how they concluded their telephone conversations. The survey listed several options, including "Bye-bye." No one thought they said "Bye-bye." But tapes of the same people talking on the phone showed that most of them did say "Bye-bye." Asked "Do you ever say 'bye-bye' at the end of a call?" the subjects all confidently claimed they never used that expression. Clearly, it is difficult to analyze your own speech. It's pretty tough to even admit to what others tell you are your speech habits. The first step in linguistic cross-training, then, is to gather samples of your own speech style. A bit of personal field study will provide information about your speech habits and favorite conversation patterns. This research requires some clever ambushing so that samples are as unstaged as possible.

YOUR VOICE MESSAGE

You can begin your field research by picking up a phone and calling your voice mailbox. Listen to the message. This isn't even a spontaneous speech sample. You probably spent a few minutes making a tape that sounded appropriate, suited to your callers, and aligned with your sense of who you are and how you do business. But do you sound confident and friendly? Or anxious, hesitant, and tentative? Do you explain the obvious ("I'm not available to take your call") or leave your caller confused ("Leave an alphanumeric message at the tone")? Do you underestimate the caller's intelligence ("State your phone number slowly and clearly") or overestimate their sense of humor (tapes with musical introductions)? Do you sound efficient ("This is Karen Stevenson. Leave me a message and I will return your call")? Or do you sound like someone without enough to do: "Hi. This is Matthew Doberman. I'm either away from my desk, in a meeting, or on another line. Your call is very important to me. Please leave a message of any length and I will call you back as soon as possible. Please speak slowly and wait for the tone. I look forward to speaking with you. Have a nice day."

You know your audience—who calls and whether they're likely to respond to an efficient message or a welcoming soliloquy. (Do avoid my least favorite message ever. It began "You have reached the number that you have dialed" and went on at a similar level of time-wasting unhelpfulness.) The point here is that a voice message is a little sample of your speech worth listening to and thinking about. You can probably draw at least one conclusion from listening: are you a person of few or many words?

QUESTIONS TO ASK YOURSELF ABOUT A VOICE MESSAGE

1. Long or short?
2. Declarative or full of questions? (Listen especially for inflected questions.)

58

3. Contextualizing: please, sorry, assurances, thank-you's?
4. Pace?
5. Confidence level?

YOUR PHONE STYLE

You can add to your research materials with a tape recorder. Phone conversations are easy to collect. If you keep a tape recorder on your desk, you can tape some samples and record your side of a conversation without permissions or breaches of confidentiality. Tape just a few minutes somewhere in the middle of a call. Try not to be conscious of the taping. Play back your little snippet, preferably the next day rather than immediately after the call. Listen to how you sound, how much you talk, how many questions you ask. You won't have any trouble remembering what the other person said if you play the tape within a day or two and you can learn a lot by revisiting what you contributed to the conversation. (You're entirely within your rights in doing this, but in a post–Linda Tripp world of paranoia, don't share your project or your tapes with anyone else. Since you're doing this taping only to gather information about yourself, you might choose to rewind to the beginning each time rather than building up a log of recordings that somebody might ask about.)

QUESTIONS ABOUT TAPED CONVERSATIONS

1. What was your goal or intention in the conversation?
2. What style or strategy did you employ: Center or Edge?
3. What was your power within this conversation—were you giving orders, asking for help, apologizing for an error, looking for feedback?
4. Did your power change as the conversation progressed?
5. Did you sound authoritative, directive, and assured? Tentative, exploratory, questioning? Did your style match your intention?

OBSERVATION

Some of the best information about my own teaching comes to me when I invite not my supervisors but my colleagues into my classroom. Peers, friends, a coworker, or a mentor can help you here. Choose someone you trust and quiz him or her about your speech habits. Ask for an informal evaluation of your standard style in a meeting or in a conversation. (You can ask for this kind of feedback in a performance review, but probably not before you've done some serious information-gathering on your own. You don't want to hand out new rulers unless you know you'll measure up.) A close pal might agree to "observe" and record for you during a conversation or meeting you both attend. If you do arrange for this kind of help, it's important to provide a guide for the observer so his feedback is worthwhile. And try not to skew your sample by being conscious of the observation. Go to the meeting, do your thing, and then see what your friend has to offer.

GUIDELINES FOR AN OBSERVATION

1. Does the speaker present information as statements or questions?
2. Does the speaker contextualize answers with disclaimers ("I'm not really sure about these figures, but . . .")?
3. Does the speaker present a confident and assured affect or does he seem nervous and hesitant?
4. Does the speaker connect her points to what's been said or take the conversation in an entirely new direction?
5. Does the speaker use evidence or experience to claim authority?
6. Does the speaker interrupt or get interrupted?
7. How often does the speaker contribute and how long is each contribution?
8. "Um" and "er": count stutters and hesitations.
9. Is there a repeated phrase ("To tell you the truth") or other habit that takes away from the speaker's effectiveness?
10. Body language:
    - Does the speaker look at individuals in the group?
    - Are his hands still or flying around?
    - Is he fidgeting or demonstrating a repeated habit of eyes or head or hands?
    - Are her facial expressions restrained or animated?
    - Does body language reinforce the conversation or undercut credibility?
11. Observe facial expressions of the listeners; gauge responses to what's being said by the listeners' faces.
12. Does gaze reinforce the power relationship in the conversation? Remember that knowledgeable speakers look directly at their audience; interested listeners acknowledge expertise with an attentive and deferential gaze.

You might agree to take turns doing this with a friend or a small group of coworkers who share an interest in the issues of speech. A colleague from your leads group might agree to visit your work and offer some feedback. You can try to "objectify" your own ears and record your own use of statement and question in a meeting. But it's hard to attend and to observe. Finally, you can always hire an executive coach or consultant to do the research for you. These people call coworkers and colleagues and then provide you with a composite profile of positive and negative feedback.

Plan to gather samples from several sources; multiple resources will give you the most reliable information. Be prepared for the fact that you may not at first accept the validity of all the feedback you gather, regardless of what means you employ. Keep digging. When you hear the same thing from several sources, believe it.

CLASSES

If your performance review or your boss directly mentions communication skills, you have a first-rate opportunity to do something organized and formal. And the company might pay for it if you show good cause for getting help. Both continuing education courses at a local college and professional development programs like those offered by the American Management Association can be useful. Even an acting or improv class will heighten your awareness of your speech habits and multiply your options.

Remember, however, the topic here is not presentation skills. No one loves the formal speech, partially because the skills and conventions involved are not those of everyday conversation. Your goal is to evaluate yourself not as a keynote speaker, but as a member of a conversation. The most useful resource would be a videotape of yourself in an unrehearsed conversation. While it's not likely that you can access this kind of resource without a lot of contrivance (or enrollment in a class or workshop), don't pass up a chance to view or create a tape if the opportunity presents itself.

DON'T PANIC

Finally, remember that you have been communicating for many years; you are already pretty savvy about this stuff. The purpose of your observation and reflection is to fine-tune the instrument, not trade it in for a cello or flugelhorn. You already make hundreds of tiny accommodations every day, drawing on a wealth of registers and styles for both business and personal conversation. A listening ear tuned to your own speech is a skill-building exercise meant to diversify your choices and increase your communication success.

LOOKING OUT

THE LANGUAGE CULTURE OF YOUR WORK

Recorded in *Liar's Poker,* Michael Lewis's transformation into a 1980s bond trader was, in part, a process of language learning. It was all about "how to make smart noises." The trader he admired most "knew how to sound as if he knew how to exploit the world's financial markets." The key words here are "sound as if." Lewis explains:

> My job was a matter of learning to think and sound like a money spinner. Thinking and sounding like Alexander [the exploiter of financial markets] were the next best thing to being genuinely talented. . . . So I listened to the master and repeated what I heard. . . . It reminded me of learning a foreign language. It all seems strange at first. Then, one day, you catch yourself thinking in the language.

Every definable group creates coherence with shared language and speech conventions. Your family has some private words and in-jokes. Your soccer team had its own nicknames; the roster read like a list of normal human beings but the locker tapes said JD, O-dog, Pass, Smack, Greener, OK, and Chainsaw. Car salesmen don't sound like social workers. Bond traders don't talk like schoolteachers—the lingo of bonds, banks, and brokers isn't the style of classrooms, children, and chalk. If you were quick to master the banker's world of fill-or-kill orders, four-cent haircuts, and road shows, you also noticed that those folks didn't sound much like the faculty at the B school. Job-based speech cultures are definable and specific.

But there's more involved than the jargon. Lewis knew there was both language and language style to learn if he was going to sound like a Salomon Brothers bond trader. He needed quick, assured answers for high-energy conversations that tolerated—even demanded—a bit of swagger. Lewis learned quickly and made a success in his new line of work. (It was probably a shock to unlearn that style when he left Salomon Brothers to become an editor at *The New York Times*.) In the world of diversification, where tobacco companies make cookies and gas pipeline companies make egg cartons, corporate mergers are complicated by these language subsets. The conventions of individual fields (or just "how we say it here") can clash as vividly with the entrepreneurs and engineers of Silicon Valley as with the French and English of Canada. Even the union of global financial giants like Deutsche Bank and Bankers Trust involve the melding of more than the businesses; communication cultures, too, have to merge effectively if the marriage is going to be a happy one.

Your next step is to give some time and thought to what constitutes the language culture of your work setting, the "foreign language" you've had to learn. Argument, for example, is tolerated to a different degree in different fields. Assertion may be expected from a lawyer but not from a therapist. Questions may be more the style of doctors and lawyers than of politicians and pundits. The Robert DeNiro–Billy Crystal film *Analyze This* builds comedy from a clash like this: the organized crime boss has never heard the word "closure" so he takes a gun to the sofa pillow when instructed to "hit something." Crystal himself tries to mimic the tough-guy language of the crime bosses when he has to pose as DeNiro's *consigliaro,* but manages only to master a slap for his partner and "You want another one?" When two offices, agencies, or departments talk about communication problems, the trouble may derive from two language cultures at odds with each other. Asking questions about the words at your work, the cash language of your job, is a good place to begin to know where you are.

QUESTIONS TO ASK ABOUT THE LANGUAGE CULTURE OF WORK

1. How do people here offer new ideas?
2. How do they offer opposing ideas or disagreement?
3. How much evidence is required and what type of evidence seems to persuade?
4. What responses do assertions elicit? What facial expressions do I see around the table when someone comes on strong with an idea? Whose words elicit nods from the chair? Whose words prompt, "Let's move on"?
5. How much personal reference is tolerated? How much emotional intensity?
6. Who gets heard? promoted? passed over? Whose name for the new program ended up on the cover sheet?

Spend time at meetings and in three- and four-way conversations both listening to the talk and also listening to the style of the talk. How are assertive statements and efforts to take on leadership received? How about claims of expertise? Watch facial expressions. Remember that claims of self-importance and authority can elicit negative responses. Such displays of experience and achievement are most readily accepted when they do not openly detract from others in the group. (If you go to a meeting and point out your own excellent results with a client, expect to ruffle a few feathers. If you openly criticize a coworker's performance, expect fur to fly. And if you add the fact that you always get to the office an hour before everyone else, plan on eating lunch alone.) Claiming experience can be the right strategy. Presenting your background through analogy is another option. Or you may choose to "bury the lead" entirely and recount your success in a giveaway: "I want to take a second here to thank Sarah. The whole Textron deal couldn't have happened if she hadn't provided all the statistics on that last conference call." Her statistics. Your deal.

MORE FIELD RESEARCH

It can be particularly enlightening to ask a few questions after a meeting. Check with your colleagues, mention the meeting, and ask, "What do you think was the most useful part of that meeting?" Then ask your boss the same question. Discover what was heard and what was remembered. Armed with this information from a variety of sources, you can figure out which presentation styles and which speech habits are the most effective in your world of work.

Your research into what's remembered should yield another benefit. We all wonder at times why we aren't heard, why our good ideas go nowhere, why our words have no impact. Talking to people about what they remember from a meeting will give you a surprising clue. Most people remember primarily what *they* said in a meeting or conversation. They actually remember very little of what was said by anyone else. This is why in *Metropolitan Life* author Fran Lebowitz says the opposite of talking isn't listening—it's waiting. Unless a surprising piece of information is delivered, it's our own idea we think about and remember best. You'll probably find that many of those inquiries about "What do you remember from our meeting" end up as efforts by your buddy or your boss to tell you—one more time—about the idea he wanted to convey at the meeting.

As you observe those who are succeeding, as you determine who gets listened to, look carefully at the upper ranks of a company. These people offer the pattern of who's likely to advance. But study the group, rather than targeting any single individual at the top. Exceptional achievement is exceptional. Successes are idiosyncratic, often unique blends of effort, circumstance, talent, chemistry, and luck—and therefore they can be hard to duplicate. Without extensive inquiry, only superficial judgments emerge. It's easy to ignore the evidence or make an invalid attribution. But it is not likely that you (or anyone else) can easily reproduce the circumstances of extraordinary success. Look at role models for general encouragement rather than for patterns to personally replicate.

Finally, pay careful attention to those who aren't heard. As a culture fascinated with achievement, we spend lots of time trying to learn from others' successes. A quick look at the latest shelf of business books confirms our obsessive interest in how this CEO or that company conquered the world. We pay little attention to failures. It's as tempting to assign a failure to stupidity (rather than looking for missing skills) as it is to see a friend's promotion as luck rather than talent. Since phenomenal achievement by definition cannot be the norm, failures are just as interesting and more instructive. Those who leave or get fired offer the best lessons about styles that don't succeed.

LOOKING IN AND LOOKING OUT: FINE-TUNING

Like Slonimsky's daughter, we speak within the context of those who speak to us. Electra learned to speak Latin with her father. She learned that English was the right choice at school. We all possess a multitude of language styles or registers that relate to the situations we confront. Choosing among them, we adapt in every conversation according to what we hear and how much we hope for the good opinion of our conversational partner. For example, in conversation with a speaker of "the Queen's English," we may begin to enunciate more clearly and mimic his or her inflections. We may slow down our conversation with a recent immigrant just mastering the language or speak to small children in a simpler way. This phenomenon is called accommodation. We listen, gather, and modify our speech all the time. The listening and learning process here isn't new and these homework assignments won't be hard. Conscious focus on looking in and looking out will heighten your awareness and teach you a lot in a very short time about your own speech style and about the cash language of your work. Listen and learn.

TRYING IN

Once you've sorted out a profile of your own standard operating procedure and a sense of the language culture of your work, you come to a critical divide:

> Two roads diverged in a wood, and I—
> I took the one less traveled by . . .

All very well and good for a poet, but if you're looking for promotion, the road less traveled may not lead to the corner office. As you look at yourself and at the world you work in, ask "How much of what I see have I comfortably adopted?" Your answer will depend on two decisions:

1. Do I find the speech style of my workplace feasible (can I pull this off)?
2. Do I find it appealing (do I want to pull this off)?

It is likely that you chose your occupation knowing what it sounded like, with some idea of the fit between who you are and the way that teachers or bankers or real estate brokers talk. As you learned the fine points and observed the details of a specific role, you made the necessary accommodations.

Where you found the role unfeasible or unattractive, you also found a roadblock to success.

Think of women in their earliest involvement in the military. The conversation they heard around them was full of sexual innuendo and laced with bawdy jokes. Not many women felt they could adopt that style of conversation and those who did confronted the social pressure to desist ("You eat with that mouth?"). Here the speech style of the workplace was, for a portion of the employees, unfeasible. Caught in a curious bind, women felt pressured to adopt language habits that social convention forbade.

More subtle is the second decision: "I can do this but do I want to?" Student teachers sometimes find that the mentors to whom they are assigned are successful teachers but not teachers the students want to mimic. They scout around looking for someone else in the department whose style fits better. Enough variety is tolerated in this field to make a wide range of individual accommodations possible; things go wrong only when the student teacher thinks Jim Carrey would be the best match! But a similar dilemma arises for trainees assigned to incompatible mentors or for workers transferred to departments where the language style conflicts with their cultural traditions. In every profession, the business of finding a speech model involves finding a feasible and an appealing pattern.

EXPERIMENTS

Once you've determined what speech strategies you'd like to acquire and can adopt with success, the best plan is to experiment in a safe environment. Copy a line or two you need to learn ("So tell me more about that" if you're already a center expert; "I disagree with that idea" if you hang out on the edge), tape it to your telephone, and try it out in a few risk-free situations. You might try making a few phone calls with a mirror on your desk to heighten your awareness and to check that your body language is supporting your words.

You might also experiment with your style at a professional conference where people don't know you well. Since language is situational, though, the situation needs to roughly match your work. Bitching out the rental car clerk isn't anything like taking your assistant to task for a shoddy report. Making demands on the phone is easier than giving an assignment in person. Small scripts and practice sentences are useful for experiments that "test the waters." The test is most likely to be a success if the topic is something you know everything about and the situation is roughly equivalent to the one you experience at work.

SCRIPTS THAT ADD LANGUAGE FROM THE CENTER

1. I disagree with that idea.
2. I would argue that . . .
3. My experience says that's a good/bad plan.
4. I'd like to look again at X (budget, time line, his qualifications, etc.).
5. I have several thoughts about how we can solve this problem.
6. I'm opposed to/in favor of that.

Memo to me: say less, sound assured, don't say "just," think *me*.

SCRIPTS THAT ADD LANGUAGE FROM THE EDGE

1. Interesting . . . go on.
2. Is there more to this issue?
3. This may not be relevant but should we consider the X (budget, time line)?
4. What else do we need to discuss?
5. What should be our plan of attack, then?
6. [Say nothing.]

Memo to me: stress inclusion, build bridges, count to three before you jump on a pause, think *we*.

TRYING OUT

This is the test. After reflection, observation, and some experimentation, integrate your new strategies into your daily work situation. If you have observed carefully, thought about your own speech and what you see around you, and practiced in a safe or small environment, you will be ready to change the mix of Language from the Center and Language from the Edge in your daily interactions at work.

PRESCRIPTIONS FOR SPEAKERS FROM THE CENTER

If you discover you are by habit likely to choose Language from the Center—if you identify with Donna Demizio or discover your boss wants you to take a listening skills workshop—here are some simple strategies you can adopt:

1. Plan the meeting to reduce your percentage of talk. If you feel you have a lot of information to deliver, consider delivering it in some format before the meeting, then devote the meeting to discussion. Precirculate or e-mail your agenda, proposal, or report, follow up by phone, hand out a summary when you arrive, and then ask for questions and comments. If everyone's done the homework, you can focus on questions about, not on a presentation of, information.
2. Prepare a list of questions that require the input of others:
   • What do you see as the unusual challenges in this project?

- What have been some of the previous problems in this area?
- What makes these initiatives work?
- What are your goals for this work?
- What more can I tell you about this?

Build questions in the second meeting from answers in the first, seeking depth rather than reviewing the same territory. Add two or three unanticipated questions—these often yield useful surprises.

3. If a key speaker pauses, say "Go on" or "That's interesting." Then shut up and see what happens. Listen.
4. Invite another speaker into the conversation, but don't ambush someone with a surprise like "Soooo, Sean, what do *you* think?" You can connect with eye contact, mention that "this relates to Sean's earlier point about cost," and see if Sean takes the bait.
5. Introduce your ideas in connection to those of others: "I like where you're going with this, Bruce, and I think . . ."
6. Relax. Allow yourself to be told. Say "Can you explain that a little more" or "I'm not sure I understand" or "Walk me through that decision."
7. Wait three seconds at a pause. Silence can produce key points.
8. Listen carefully. Try not to think about what you want to say next. Take notes to force yourself to focus on others' words.
9. Give particular attention to whatever is said in the final five minutes of the meeting. A salient point may be added when it's now or never. Listen like crazy at the very end of a meeting or conversation. Comfort is often at its high point and unguarded comments are gold.
10. Just shut up.

PRESCRIPTIONS FOR SPEAKERS FROM THE EDGE

What if you feel more connected to Andrew Godfrey than to Donna Demizio? Here are some simple strategies for speakers who feel stuck in Language from the Edge:

1. Before you go to a meeting, figure out what's the real agenda and the likely topics of discussion. Do your homework, but keep most of it in your notebook. Think of it as part of your confidence rather than something you have to deliver or prove you did. Formulate two or three pieces of information you want to convey and give some thought about how to present them briefly and clearly. Ask yourself why these points are important. Are they important to the group or only to you? Can they be formulated positively and in a way that neither criticizes nor embarrasses key people at the meeting? "I think we need a separate Web site for this division" is not as effective as "What we've already done with technology in this division makes a Web site the next logical step . . . and I think Micrographics can do for us what they did for HR."

2. Ideas do not sell themselves. Once you've developed a point you want to make or a plan you want to propose, lobby for your idea. You can succeed if you've refined and tested your idea with a few colleagues or run it by your boss. You can "borrow" authority if the right person supports your idea. (You eliminate tentative language and wordy evidence when you know in advance that your idea will be well received.)

3. Be concise. Make your point clearly and briefly. End with a period not a question. Expect some opposition and return to your point if you're committed to the value of the idea. "Sell the call."

4. Establish authority. You may have to build from a small niche of expertise, but find a strength and develop it. Offer a context for your idea that lends credibility. Re-

member the power of analogy, the specific piece of evidence, the "opposite" claim.

5. Think about timing. Meetings often begin with a lot of jockeying for position and gestures meant to reestablish the power structure. Hang back a little. Strong, new ideas that get lost at the beginning of the agenda can fare better in the middle. Since most people are waiting to talk rather than listening to other speakers' ideas, complicated ideas may not be heard at all their first time out. Reiterate your ideas. (You might want to repeat and rephrase a good idea you heard early in the meeting; you'll probably get the credit for it!)

6. Don't be afraid to disagree. With an alternative answer or plan, you're not disagreeing with another person; you're disagreeing with another idea. Likewise, don't take personally the rejection of your idea by others.

7. Don't undercut your words with canceling body language or disclaimers. If you're always tapping a pencil when you talk, people will remember the pencil. Sit still, look at your audience, don't grimace. Avoid intensity; neutrality complements authority.

8. Be friendly, assured, and reserved. People are best able to focus on your ideas when you don't distract them with personal information. Don't support an increased estimate of Gillette's earnings with a story about your husband's shaving habits.

9. Finally, remember this is called *work*. Expect to hear comments and criticisms of your ideas. Expect a meeting to be a political arena. Be tough. It's like membership in an Internet chat room: if you lurk, you will never get flamed but you'll never be heard either. Your ideas will survive best if you test-drive them before you present them and if you align them with shared goals within the group. Innovations that solve acknowledged problems (not just your favorite gripe) are the most likely to be heard.

MAKE HASTE SLOWLY

As you try out new styles, observe your own experience. Cross-examine conversations that fail and determine what factors of language—and what other factors—were involved. Reflection is good. You can often rethink an interview that died or a conversation that failed or a deal that cratered and find out more about why.

In his comprehensive study *An Introduction to Sociolinguistics,* linguist Ronald Wardhaugh writes: "'power' is a useful concept that will help explain much linguistic behavior. Power, as both something to achieve and something to resist, exerts considerable influence on the language choices that many people make." Thinking about the power dynamics of a situation can guide you in choosing a speech style that matches your intention—to take power or to accept and enhance the power of others. Try some of these strategies. Experiment with change. And know that big changes aren't required. You're not learning Mandarin or even cultivating a British accent. Language learning is continuous, largely unconscious, and recursive. You're actually making changes all the time. Go ahead—affect the situations you confront as well as react to them. If "War is politics by other means," then work and its daily politics are war by other means. This is war. You want to win. There will be costs. Choose your battles—and your weapons.

REVIEW

Look In: What is my speech style?
Look Out: What is the speech style of my work culture?
Try In: What speech habits can I successfully adopt and add to my own?
Try Out: Where can I successfully integrate some of these new techniques?

A LAST WORD

Remember that most work requires both language styles. Choosing carefully is your goal. Demizio's and Godfrey's only mistake is that they don't change gears. Demizio takes over every interaction. Godfrey turns every conversation into an interview. The ideal for both of them is the same: direct when you can and step back when you should. If you've done your homework and know what your most comfortable speech style is, you can broaden your range with strategies from another style. But keep as much variety and flexibility in your responses as possible. No one way is right. A range of weapons is your best defense.

CHAPTER FOUR
PUTTING LANGUAGE TO WORK

When Donna Demizio received her performance review, her boss, Larry Evans, identified this area of concern:

> I feel like she's all over every meeting we have and the client never gets to talk about the problems . . . the unusual constraints. Then the whole thing craters because there was this big, important thing we didn't know.

In the conversation that followed, Evans tried to explain the problem to Demizio:

> You're doing a lot of business for us. We love that. But there are deals that fall apart near the end of the process, deals that everyone thought were locked up. Why didn't Alliance come through? What happened with ERT? You spent a ton of time on both of those. We're worried when projects fall apart right before

they're signed. A lot of time is wasted and it seems like we're always getting blindsided at the last minute.

The other thing is your team. They love you to death, Donna, but they're feeling pushed around. I can't have Al and Matt and Jen in here every other day telling me about this problem and that problem. You've got to find ways to deal with this yourself. I can't be baby-sitting your people. I've got fifty-three people in this office and, honestly, I don't want to talk to every one of them every day.

To Demizio, Evans's explanation sounds like a demand for more work. He wants more deals. He wants Demizio to take more responsibility for her team. What about the six million dollars in sales? How can Evans be asking for more work than that? Demizio already feels maxed-out. This conversation seems like a bad dream.

W. H. Auden wrote, "We would rather be ruined than changed." As she leaves Evans's office, Demizio's first reaction is to muscle her clients into submission and whip her team into shape. Not surprisingly, she wants to attack these problems with her standard directive style. If all you have is a hammer, every problem looks like a nail. But you can't solve new problems with old tools. A little cross-training will let her work smarter, not harder.

She's not exactly enthusiastic, however, about Language from the Edge:

What, are you crazy? I can't do that. I'll sound like a wimp. I'll never get anything done if I have to sit there and listen to those people go on forever. . . . Evans doesn't know what it's like out there. He hasn't been in the field in five years. I'm not going to get anywhere by changing my voice mail message.

78

Demizio isn't likely to stop using Language from the Center as her core style of doing business. And for the most part, her standard method of operation is working. But the tough competition in her industry and a performance review that sounded like "work harder" eventually persuaded her to give Language from the Edge a try.

Look In

Using the program outlined in Chapter 3, Demizio should start by looking in and looking out.

1. Taping a few of her own phone calls will start her thinking about how she sounds and how much she listens.
2. A day out of the office making calls with a colleague in a different industry can provide breathing space and a chance to observe, compare, and think about style.
3. Sitting in on a colleague's team meeting might inspire some comparative thinking.

Look Out

For Demizio, important information lies in the deals that didn't happen. If the recurrent problem in those deals was information that she forgot to uncover, never heard, or didn't remember, then Language from the Edge can help.

1. It's easy to blame lost deals on price. But Office Creations, like most vendors, has an array of price points. Price doesn't kill deals at the eleventh hour unless a key player in the decision was overlooked. Deals are dismantled by inaccurate information, inadequacies in the proposal, or a plan that doesn't match the clients' vision. If Demizio can ask more questions and listen to her clients, she's less likely to lose them.

2. It's crucial to attribute failures to the right causes. Demizio needs to call, ask, dig—cross-examine conversations for credibility. Was that answer just a way to get off the hook, or does it make sense? She should ask a second round of questions the next time she sees her contact. Or solicit her boss's involvement. If Evans wants Demizio to improve, her problems are his problems. Getting good information about what fails and what succeeds with your clients is essential for making the right changes.

3. Jim Carrey's *Liar Liar* begins with the perky assurance and unremitting duplicity we often associate with lawyers. Carrey greets colleagues, family, and friends with his signature smile, a polished appearance, and a solid belief that other people are good for what you can get out of them. This fast-talking liar is a stereotype of self-interest, a vision every salesperson has to combat. Demizio and her colleagues can't establish the credibility of neutrality with a commission hanging over their heads. A speech style that directs the conversation and sounds like an enumeration of projects and experience may raise the image of a fast-talking trickster with a "treat-'em and street-'em" agenda. The listening, indirection, and inclusivity of Language from the Edge can help Demizio counter negative perceptions about people on commission or anyone with a vested interest behind his pitch.

TRY IN AND OUT

1. Demizio should try Language from the Edge on a new client whose decision process is fairly straightforward. A repeat client would offer the security of previous success; however, the familiar account is more likely to greet changes with surprise: "What's going on, Donna? You sound like a goddamn therapist or something."

2. Her goal throughout the initial contacts is to reduce the

percentage of Donna-talk and make the client talk as much as possible. Once she gets to the bid stage, prepared materials can reduce her temptation to talk. Armed with a good proposal, she can begin her presentation with "Now remind me, what are the critical goals and parameters of this project?" The key decision-maker is the one most likely to respond to this question. Thus Demizio can focus on drawing out this speaker's point of view.

3. The three-second rule can help: when a speaker pauses, Demizio should count to three before she responds. Silence breeds information. (You've seen the corollary to this on *Sally* and *Oprah*: a couple declares their marriage a success, elaborates on a few minor problems, and gets ambushed by "Is there anything else you're holding back?" The next thing you know, all the dirty laundry is hanging out to dry and half the audience is in tears.) Wait patiently for information to emerge. Ask if there's more to tell.

4. Wherever there is power, there is resentment. If Demizio is a team leader, there will be some abrasiveness over her direction. But listening to the team, responding to what they have to say, and asking questions can build rapport. In an experiment with her team, small changes are a good way to begin. Power that listens has the best survival rate.

5. With her team, Demizio might reduce her Language from the Center by presenting the week's projects or policies by listserver e-mail. At the regular meetings, then, the focus can be on the power of ideas: "What can make us a better team?" or "What's happening" as reported by each member of the team. Demizio can also present a shared problem and ask the team to offer input for the solution. She should plan time for "new business," that part of every agenda that usually evaporates as people are putting away their notes and wondering if the cafeteria is still open.

6. Since Evans views the team's complaints as significant—he wouldn't have listened if they were unimportant—

Demizio should also run her overall plan by her boss, asking Evans for feedback about the proposed changes. Keeping Evans "in the loop" shows what Demizio is doing to solve the problem and also coopts his support.

With a little reflection and a little practice, Demizio can adopt scripts and habits that will give her clients and her team more time to talk, more input into the work they share, and more respect for her way of working with them. With cooperation from Evans and some touch-base conversations, Demizio can also coopt her boss into this new initiative.

Andrew Godfrey didn't like his performance review either:

> Increased directness in all areas would result in greater management confidence. . . . A lack of directness leads to the perception that Andrew is unable to form an opinion or communicate it well.

Godfrey is upset:

> Listen, these are serious issues. Folks need to see the whole picture in order to understand what's at stake. You can't reduce this stuff to twenty-five words or less. I sincerely wish I could.

Like Demizio, Godfrey feels his work is being attacked. David Callen, his boss, seems to be doubting his competence: "unable to form an opinion." That hurts. Godfrey's response, like Demizio's, is to hunker down in the very position he's been criticized for and try to explain why change is not going to work. However, Language from the Center can improve Godfrey's situation and make his performance review a prescription about speech style rather than an attack on his professional expertise. After all, Callen doesn't think Godfrey is a poor environmental lawyer; he just wants to keep the CEO happy. If Godfrey recognizes the conflict of speech cultures inherent in this situation—the lawyers who need to get everything right versus the managers who need to get everything done—he will see the value of a different style of conversation when he meets with the corporate leaders. The request is not for a change of personality, just a change of speech style.

LOOK IN

Godfrey can continue to protect the company and still adopt Language from the Center as an overlay to his own more responsive style.

1. Watching himself in the mirror during phone calls can help Godfrey speak with assurance and eliminate facial expressions of doubt or tentativeness.
2. Taping and listening to his side of phone calls will determine how often he asks questions and how often he offers brief, directive answers.

LOOK OUT

1. Like Demizio, Godfrey should enlist the aid of Callen in his experiments. If he knows the CEO's goal before each meeting, he can tailor his comments accordingly and work with the grain of the meeting rather than against it.
2. Scheduling a few lunches with some corporate contacts or attending a conference with a management slant might help Godfrey think productively about different styles of speaking.

TRY IN AND OUT

1. A next step for Godfrey might be an intradepartmental meeting with an agenda and an adjournment time. A lis-

tening and inclusive style doesn't mean meetings can't have a framework and a focus.

2. At meetings with senior management, Godfrey should offer short answers, with the suggestion of more information available on request: "I can explain the trade-offs and risks if you'd like, but what I think we should do is . . ." Claiming his authority and making his point firmly will inspire confidence. An analogy to a parallel situation will underline the fact that there are no easy answers: "I think this has the potential to be another Three Mile Island. We need to proceed with caution." A detailed follow-up memo or a report to the decision-makers can cover issues too complicated for the CEO's pace.

3. Godfrey's knowledge of environmental law is the basis of his expertise. If he does the homework, it doesn't necessarily need to be "turned in," that is, reported—it just needs to be readily available if questions arise. Brief points—"horseback answers"—will serve Godfrey best with his CEO.

4. Besides premeeting conversations with Callen to identify the desired outcome of a meeting, Godfrey can further build his power base if he can research and endorse the CEO's vision, agenda, and motivation. An occasional informal conversation with the CEO will help both people relax and understand the other's position.

ADDING, NOT TAKING AWAY

Are Godfrey and Demizio likely to transform their personalities? No—nor should they. Are they selling out to some alien and inauthentic change? Hardly. They're adding tools. When you have more than a hammer, you can deal with things other than nails. And while working from the edge will help Demizio fine-tune her contracts and work with her team, she's not likely to want to give up the core style that brought in six million dollars this year. Low-energy silence isn't in her future, but small changes can make her more efficient and more productive. The same applies to Godfrey. He will probably see the directive style of Language from the Center as feasible, but, as a legal adviser, he will balk at swallowing it whole. Change in the right settings, however, can give him credibility with management (and will definitely make his meetings shorter).

WHEN CHANGE CAN'T HAPPEN

Professor Hilary Lane teaches at one of the country's top business schools and her classes are among the most popular. She is a charismatic speaker as well, and when she talks about econometrics, the numbers dance. She is on everybody's list of interesting people and first-class thinkers. Students line up early for her office hours, cluster around her after class, and fight for time in her schedule of conference appearances, corporate consulting, interview requests, and TV appearances. Early on, Lane found she was "a person who can't say 'no.'" She wanted to help and was happy to talk to everyone who had an interesting idea to share. She was intrigued by every project that came her way—and she was exhausted.

She resolved to say "no" a lot more. She promised herself to make her conversations brief and to make clear to her many petitioners the limits of her time. But it didn't work. Her students were, after all, the reason she was at the business school. And the phone calls, clients, and inquiries were important to her, the source of many of her case studies. Finally, as a teacher, her work culture—the world of academia—encouraged the donation of limitless time to her students, her colleagues, in fact, to anyone who asked for it. So Lane hired someone to say "no" for her. Barbara Agnelli keeps Lane's book, schedules her meetings, and treats everyone with exactly the same intense interest and listening attention that Lane is known for. But when you get off the phone with Agnelli, you still don't have an appointment with Lane. You've been noticed and encouraged and listened to. But Agnelli won't let Lane schedule anything be-

yond what her open time blocks will accommodate. Lane hasn't changed who she is, but she's assigned what she doesn't do easily to someone else. It seems to keep almost everyone happy and now Lane goes home before 10 P.M.

As described in Chapter 3, a speaker considering change evaluates both the attractiveness and feasibility of that change. Demizio may want to work from the edge, but she isn't going to give away client presentations. Taking on an intern or a university work-study student in the marketing or business program are options. A junior person to handle the homework might free Demizio to listen and probe more. With Godfrey, it's answers and experience that he's paid for. But team members can put together postmeeting support material to cover the risks and trade-offs alluded to in the meetings. Not all the answers need to be given in full in the conference room.

Sometimes, what we need to do is beyond our range. But sometimes, we can hire or find someone else to fill in the gaps.

NOT A COMMUNICATION PROBLEM

What if department politics are involved? What if Demizio is just being chastised as a motor-mouthed woman? (Gloria Steinem has said that women are seen as talkative only because the desired model for their behavior is silence.) What if Callen wants to get rid of Godfrey? (Maybe the CEO wants to promote a rising star in the department.) Alas, "communication skills" is vague enough to bear the burden of almost any kind of gripe. If these issues aren't real, time will reveal the true motivations behind the assessments. This year's problem with communication will become next year's problem with professionalism or deadlines or team spirit. However, both Demizio and Godfrey, in adding useful speech skills and in getting their bosses' involvement, are demonstrating a commitment to their work, to performance goals, and to their clients and teams. They'll eventually find out if other factors are at work (see Sharon Post's story at the end of this chapter), but their intervening time and efforts are still of value.

In the end, every speaker should be able to work from the center and from the edge, according to his or her situation. One speech style is going to feel like home territory. But the other is a useful option. Continue to listen and think about your own style and the styles you see around you. You already know 90 percent of what it takes to get your job done. Keep the language of power and the language of influence in your toolbox. As you talk your way through the day, sort out the power structures and decide whether you are best served by taking control, directing the conversation, and claiming the right to do so—or by listening, asking questions, and teasing out and collecting the power of ideas.

OTHER CASES

A SMALL PROBLEM: THE RENTAL COUNTER

The FBI training courses for embassy diplomats suggest that if you are kidnapped by terrorists, your best bet is to shut up, do what you're told, and stay calm. Police officers facing down an assailant with a deadly weapon choose "Sir, I believe you have a weapon. I am asking you to drop that weapon now, sir" rather than "Drop that goddamn gun before I blow your face off."

Language can create power but it is also determined by power. What should you do when you have absolutely no power whatsoever? Can you work from the edge and still accomplish your goal?

Only ten minutes behind your ETA, you arrive at the car rental desk to find an agent looking quizzically into her computer display screen while an agitated young woman taps her fingers on the Formica. "No, they quoted me $95 over the phone," the customer says. The agent performs a little burst of typing and stands bemused before the display screen. "It's $125."

"No, they quoted me $95 over the phone," the customer firmly intones.

The agent performs another little burst of typing. "It's $125," she says.

You get the idea—it's a lather/rinse/repeat scenario and everyone's going nowhere fast. Another customer arrives at the desk with a folder in her hand. She sizes things up. She paces a bit. She tries to make eye contact with someone. She looks around the desk to see if there's another agent in the area. Then she sighs like an elephant chained in the sun. You'd like to assert yourself and say, "Please finish this transaction immediately and attend to me before this antsy elephant cuts the line!" But you have no power. Talking tough might produce some results, but those results would include three instant enemies, one of whom has your car keys.

Because you have no power here, Language from the Edge is the best choice. Think *we*. Ask the finger-tapping customer, "Is there another agent around?" You're not distracting the rental agent or criticizing her. You're suggesting she deserves help. Then try a team strategy: "We all want to get out of here but there's only one of you [eye contact with the agent]. Is there anything we can do to move things along?"

When I used this strategy, I kept my blood pressure down, I made no enemies, the agent said, "I'm almost done," Person No. 3 announced she only wanted to turn in her paperwork (the agent took her folder and she left), and the young woman ahead of me said, "Okay . . . just go with the $125 and I'll get Travel to sort it out." Three minutes later, I had my car keys! Working from the edge gave everyone a chance to respond. Since we all shared the same problem, collaboration worked. Working from the edge can be the best route when you have no power to change or escape your situation.

A Medium Problem: The Boss

Emlyn Anderson's boss, Jack Lanzo, told her she was going to be a great addition to Ahern Architectural Associates. An expert in computer design programs, she was hired so Ahern could expand its project roster. Three months into the job, Anderson finds things aren't going very well. In the open office format at Ahern, Lanzo's desk is fifteen feet from Anderson's work station and whenever a colleague approaches to ask Anderson a question, Lanzo comes over to see what's going on or looks up from his desk and says, "What's the problem?"

Anderson feels like she can't build power if she never gets to speak for herself. But she isn't sure how to silence her boss. If she turns to Lanzo and says, "I can handle this," will he fire her?

This is a situation where Language from the Center can help. "I can handle this" doesn't need to be delivered like a slap.

With confidence and a sense that these are the things Lanzo hired her for, it should be the right response.

What if Lanzo gets up anyway and comes over? What if he continues to micromanage her work? Then Language from the Edge might be her next strategy. She might actively solicit Lanzo's input about her next project. By approaching him with a question, she can signal her respect for his expertise and his time in the profession. Gathering his wisdom and counsel at the beginning of an assignment will help Anderson look good and Lanzo let go. And once she's shown she respects him, he may start to do the same for her.

If, after this, Lanzo persists in undercutting her, it's unlikely that any specific speech strategies can solve the problem. Anderson's problem may be complicated by gender, race, education, or age issues. Nonetheless, she should continue to answer questions with authority and convey an affect of control. She may have to say to Lanzo, "You just answered a question that was addressed to me." Or ask coworkers to e-mail their questions. But if the problem persists, she's going to have to move her desk or look for a different assignment.

A BIG PROBLEM: CONFLICTING SPEECH CULTURES

A clash of language styles shouldn't require professional translators. But when corporate cultures collide, it can sound like the Tower of Babel. Such was the story of the attempted union of Alma Mater University's library and its information technology department.

Early in 1996, guided by a California consulting firm, AMU merged its Memorial Library with the information systems department to create Information Resources (IR). Budgets were blended. To oversee the marriage, a new position was created: vice president for information resources. Like Adam in the Garden of Eden, the new VP asserted control by naming everything. He set up a hierarchical structure entirely antithetical to the style and history of libraries but also unfamiliar to the world of information systems and computing. In the library, he eliminated the reference department, the cataloging unit, acquisitions, interlibrary loan, and circulation. In the computing area, he eliminated the networking group, the user services group, and the help desk. Since everything had a new name, a kind of IR-speak evolved. Conversations seemed at cross-purposes. Even the provost's college-wide announcement of the change was circulated by e-mail only. Forty employees were reassigned to six information teams—the response team, the training team, the new initiatives team, delivery, selection, and planning. The linguistic revision marked the enormity of the changes. The library and the IS department, each with its own culture, ties, rituals, affiliations, and language styles, lost discrete identity. It took a year to implement the reconfiguration and another year and a half for it to fully fail.

The library people saw their job as educational. They defined themselves and their interactions as instructional and they spoke from the edge, listening to patrons, facilitating the work of others. They worked in close affiliations, valued process, and asked lots of questions. (They also preferred order, security, and plants on the sunny windowsills.) The computer people were more instrumental in both their behavior and their speech style. They preferred to do things for users, seeing most problems and questions as one-time issues. Solitary problem-solvers, anxious to accomplish quick information delivery and move on, they valued output and directive statements. (They preferred speed, door keys for everybody, and pizza boxes on the windowsills.) The librarians thought the IS people were unhelpful, closemouthed, and proprietary about information. IS thought the librarians talked too much.

"Marry in haste, repent at leisure." The failed union of these two departments might be a case study in the anthropology of work. Each department had its own way of operating, its own rules, and its own language habits. If the librarians found the computer people abrupt and dictatorial, the computer staff felt

91

the library people asked too many questions. A fuller understanding of the work of each department would have benefited both groups, as would a little training around language issues. If Information Systems thought about responsive scripts, they might have made librarians more comfortable. If librarians hadn't approached IS like patrons in need of assistance, they might have retained more control. Turf wars, personalities, and logistics were undoubtedly part of the problem. But the communication styles of the two departments aggravated every other issue.

WHEN IT'S NOT ABOUT SPEECH STYLE

Sharon Post, an assistant product manager for a large brokerage house, oversees the investment analysts' communication with the sales force. She is involved in every aspect of information dissemination and she is in charge of scheduling the "morning call," a daily report to sales by research personnel. The job requires both organizational skills and a fine diplomacy: every analyst thinks he or she should be on the call but only six or seven analysts speak each day. Gatekeeping is the challenge in Post's job. She is always saying "no" to people who make four times what she does (and who figure a few good appearances on the call could make that into five times as much as she does!). About 80 percent of Post's work is done on the phone. Last year, Post's performance review suggested she take speech training; several sales people and three analysts complained that Post "always bites my head off" or "sounds too bitchy."

Post dutifully headed off to twice-weekly sessions with a speech coach who taught her to round her vowels and to speak from the diaphragm. She did the breathing exercises and, between brushing and flossing, read the practice lists aloud into her bathroom mirror. The performance review provided the motivation. But when Post tried her new skills in the office, two different salesmen asked her if she was trying to fake a

British accent, her assistant asked her why she was acting so "stuck up," and her boyfriend didn't recognize her voice on the phone. Post found she was able to make the suggested changes, but she didn't like the result. She began to think more about her interactions with analysts. She noticed that the analysts who were (for various reasons) afraid for their jobs were the most likely to "go off on me" or get huffy when she couldn't fit them in. She also noticed that several of these people were able to successfully appeal the schedule to her boss. Her boss often reversed her decisions, bending rules she was supposed to enforce.

Post's problems weren't about speech or speech styles. Her problems were inherent in her job of saying "no" to powerful people and in her boss's failure to back her decisions. She dropped the voice lessons and negotiated the daily schedule so that her job was to post the names of all those who had asked to appear. Her boss, a managing director, took over final approval. She's never heard anything more about speech lessons.

CONCLUSION

Even experts make mistakes. When my Web site was under construction, I corresponded with the builders by e-mail. I was still a novice at html and made the mistake of working from the edge when I should have been in the center. As pages of the site were posted, I was horrified to see glaring typos, the kind of thing that writers take seriously. My credibility was about to evaporate in a very public setting. I tapped out an e-mail to my Web site assistant: "You do proofread this stuff, don't you?"

"No," he typed back. I got my answer—I should never have asked a question. The original message should have read: "Ian, do not post any pages that haven't been thoroughly proofread for accuracy and correctness."

Live and learn. Age, gender, and expertise all figured into this scenario. But Language from the Center would have been a better strategy. We all need to know how to follow our dance partner but also how to lead. Begin by increasing your awareness of your speech habits. *What do I sound like? How do I approach a problem? Do I prefer to work from the center or the edge?* Consider the world of your work. Observe the successful people and those who get heard. *Do statements work better than questions? Do claims of expertise bolster authority? Are contrarian statements noticed?* Learn from what you observe, plan your strategy for the next meeting, and experiment with change. Multiply your options. Develop scripts for difficult situations. And look for the balance of mirror and mold that language takes in every conversation, reflecting what's going on but also what's useful in changing the shape of the situation. Finally, watch out for personality conflicts and performance problems that are packaged as language issues. It's easy to call anything a communication problem. But most people who say "You're not listening to me," really mean "You're not doing what I want you to do!"

CHAPTER FIVE

TRANSITIONS

A hundred years ago, George Bernard Shaw's *Pygmalion*—the source of Lerner and Lowe's popular musical *My Fair Lady*—explored the transformation of Eliza Doolittle, a poor London flower girl "condemned by every syllable she utters." But with instruction in the dialect and deportment of the upper class, Eliza eventually passed herself off as a princess. The change came with a hefty price tag in the area of identity, but Eliza's story offers a good lesson in the power of words to change circumstances. The Harrison Ford–Melanie Griffith film *Working Girl* tells the same story with a modern spin—this time the Eliza character aspires to the corporate "upper class." When the boss is hospitalized, Griffith seizes the opportunity to present herself as more than a secretary. In her debut, Griffith almost gives herself away by interpreting the invitation for "Coffee?" as a command to go make some. But with the help of careful observation, a lot of homework, and her boss's voice tapes, she ultimately passes as an investment-banker-in-training.

Language, a useful tool in all our daily transactions, is particularly important when we make a work transition. My own fascination with this phenomenon grew out of work with student teachers. I have supervised people of every age in their training as secondary school teachers and there are many challenges in this learning process. One of the most consistent is the fact that most novice teachers are experts in their subject but not yet expert teachers. The apprentice eleventh-grade American history teacher knows everything there is to know about presidents, politics, and policy. But she's not an expert teacher. Her mastery of wars, elections, and the Constitution isn't going to help the first time a student raises a hand to ask, "Do we have to know this?"

Training teachers in the psychology of education, in the sociology of schools, and in the techniques of educational research is part of the work. But sounding like a teacher is what gets you through the first few days. Marco Butera, for example, knew he had to maintain order and he tried "Excuse me, is there something you need to say?" and "Ben, could you pay attention?" He quickly found that asking questions led to answers and often his students would respond with "Well, yes, there is . . . why are we doing this?" or with some other attempt to divert the class (Ben responded with "I need to get a drink"). In time, Butera took a more directive approach ("Quiet down" or just "*Ben*"). But in order to present the basis of his expertise as a teacher, Butera needed to create the control and credibility of an experienced teacher. Learning the right speech style gave him the time and space to accumulate expertise.

Because language is so closely connected to identity, however, resistance is usually part of transformation. We already witnessed this response in Demizio's and Godfrey's reactions to their performance reviews. It is natural to cling to old ways of doing things. Most student teachers don't like the move from one side of the desk to the other, from the responsive mode to the directive one. They try to be friends with their students for a while; soon they recognize that friendship is not the most useful gift a teacher can make to a student.

Job transitions—new job or new company—benefit when speech style is considered as part of the change. It's nice to imagine that you can just go on being your old self. After all, it was that old self that was selected for the new position. But you can understand your new work and also enhance your success if you take into account speech styles and the language of your work culture.

A First Job

> 1. At the beginning, expect to work from the edge. 2. Begin as a sponge. 3. Look for new ground. 4. Borrow power.

Peter Smith majored in political science and, on graduation, headed off to Wall Street. He landed a job with a well-known bank and was assigned to asset management. "For the first six months, I was a human sponge," says Smith. "I listened and learned and kept my mouth shut." Since Smith was a new hire, no one expected him to do otherwise. "And I was so junior," he adds, "I figured if I asked a dumb question, there wasn't very far for me to fall." Working from the edge—asking questions, encouraging others to talk—Smith set an appropriately deferential tone for his questions and kept the information coming.

Smith was particularly lucky that his job was in a new area for the company. The asset management department was a start-up operation and Smith was its only trainee. He was new, but so was the department. Getting noticed is easier if you're solving an acknowledged problem or breaking new ground. Joining a new initiative at the firm gave Smith both these elements. He didn't have to break through an old guard of established players and he didn't have to accommodate the "how we've always done it" mentality. When he saw a chance to make things better, his bosses listened to his questions. His energy and commitment were particularly valuable because his job was part of a planned innovation. Even now, Smith always says "we" rather than "I." He presents a new idea with "What if we . . ." This conditional phrasing doesn't sound much like the bond traders on the eleventh floor who prefer "That's wrong" or "Dump the whole lot and do it yesterday." But if Language from the Edge doesn't sound like a Master of the Universe, it still serves Smith well. He's not expected to know everything and his colleagues understand that, for the good of the start-up, he needs to be helped.

Fortunately, the bank is a flat organization that endorses the team approach. Smith realized this in the interview process: he met with eighteen different people, all of whom had input, either written or oral, in his hiring. "They want everyone you'll work with, everyone you might even have a chance of working with, involved in the hiring," says Smith. "I was pretty sure I wouldn't have to hunt down a mentor . . . I knew that everyone would be part of my learning process." The human sponge acknowledges the help he's gotten and trades against it. "My first rule is to give credit where it's due—even when only a little of it is due—to those who have helped me," Smith confides. "In this way, I take on the stature of those around me."

For the time being, Smith doesn't have to compete with other new hires within asset management. He only needs to do his job well. Establishing competence early is important. If Smith is viewed as hard-working and able, his assignments will be more important. If he puts in the time, produces good results, and gives credit where it's due, he is also likely to receive the best mentoring available. Over time, advantages accumulate and a strong beginning starts the trajectory to later successes. Smith recognizes that such achievement, however, is time-consuming. If he wants to do his job well, he's going to have to work. So there's nothing he won't do—wear a beeper, drive the books out to Newark Airport on New Year's Day, stay until midnight on a Saturday night. No problem. And if something goes wrong? "I'm happy to be the piñata," says Smith. "If you want me to, I'll even bring the candy."

Smith is off to a good start. He's observed carefully the culture of his work; he's committed to learning the business, the lingo, and the speech style of an asset management banker as it is practiced at his bank. As the new kid on the block, he uses the human sponge strategy—the listening, responding, and questioning style of Language from the Edge—to master these lessons. Language from the Edge is also the right choice for this team-management organization and for a financial field where thoroughness, care, counseling, and trust are central to success.

BACK TO WORK

> 1. Learn the lingo. 2. Establish an area of significant specialization.

Judy Sedlar joined American Airlines after her last child went to college. Sedlar's six weeks of training in Dallas focused on a thick curriculum of service routines and FAA regulations, as well as a long list of emergency and safety procedures. In the process, Sedlar also learned the lore and the lingo: how to bid a line (request certain work days and flights), trip-trade (modify her schedule), preplot (plan choices off the computer), and max out by the seventeenth (finish the legally allowed hours for the month). Over time she learned who was a senior momma (female flight attendant with many years of service), who was a slam-clicker (attendants who don't socialize in the destination cities), and how to choreograph a meal and a follow-on (snack) in the narrow space of the aft galley on a transcon. But just learning how to smile all the time didn't create any particular power in her new career. In fact, on most of the transcons, surrounded by experienced crew, Sedlar watched carefully, tried to stay out of the way, and worked from the edge.

Three weeks into this life and on a flight to California, Sedlar answered an attendant call button from a young mother with an infant daughter who had been intermittently crying and fussing since takeoff. The mother herself was now on the verge of tears. She was taking her first child to see her grandparents on the Coast and she was sure the baby was seriously ill. "She was fine all week—I don't know what's wrong—but I'm sure she's got a raging fever and I don't have any medications with me . . . I can't let her be this sick with three more hours to fly!" The other attendants, experienced but mostly in their late twenties, gathered around, trying to keep things under control. They hoped this wasn't going to be a crisis. Sedlar asked if the mother had a thermometer (no). Then she asked if she might hold the baby for a moment (yes). She put the baby's face up to her own cheek. She heard herself saying, with the voice of practiced assurance, "I'm guessing your daughter's not in perfect health but she doesn't have a fever. She's probably got a cold . . . although the fussiness may just be from pressure changes, inner ear discomfort. You said she was fine this morning. Let's give her something to suck on—a bottle, a pacifier—and see how she does." Suddenly the accumulated knowledge of twenty years of mothering gave Sedlar expertise and respect. And her fever test had both the ring of credibility and the power to calm. Things quieted down—so did the baby.

Sedlar has been flying with American for about a year now. Like Smith, Sedlar was, at first, busy listening and learning because she was the acknowledged junior person on every flight. Things are a little different now. A significant area of expertise that is value-added on Sedlar's flights distinguishes her from the other junior flight attendants. Because it's easy to respect people we find knowledgeable (particularly if they convey that knowledge in a friendly way), Sedlar's experiences as a parent give her special status. As a mom and as a walking fever thermometer, she's handy to have around. And her talents don't make her coworkers look less able. When she works a flight, Sedlar uses Language from the Edge with most of the passengers and Language from the Center when she needs to take control. And when the new hires assume she's a senior momma, she doesn't say a thing.

A New Job

> 1. Stay flexible. 2. Blend new work with old expertise.

Bill Serruto spent eleven years waiting to make partner at a prestigious financial house. A merger shook him out and he landed in a small money management endeavor halfway across the country. In a two-person office (with two support staff) in a strip mall in Evanston, Illinois, he feels like he just drew the Candyland card that says "Go Back to the Molasses Swamp."

Serruto's not exactly starting all over again, but the transition is more complicated than just being "a human sponge." In his former job, Serruto was assigned to pitch deals and he hopped, on command, from project to project. "I was assigned by central staff to do a pitch or run a meeting, and my work was essentially reactive," says Serruto. "Thirty, forty guys calling me every day, a lot of travel, unpredictability, three airline tickets in my pocket and a settled destination only when I checked my voice mail in the cab on the way to the airport. I was supposed to keep clients happy and persuade them we were focused on them." He talked a conciliatory line, listened to people get mad, coddled everyone along, kept the deals alive, and used a lot of subjunctives ("If that were to happen," "I wish that were the case").

Serruto's new employer, Eric Liebert, liked Serruto's energy and experience. Liebert wanted a smart guy to do the things he hated. "Eric is a strategist . . . he hates meetings," says Serruto.

"He'd rather think. It's my job to find the clients, bring in investors, hunt down the money."

When Serruto reads the *Wall Street Journal* every morning, he remembers how far away New York is and he pauses over the tombstones (stock-offering announcements) that feature his former employer's name. He hasn't quite gotten past wishing for the immediate death of the guy who got his partnership. And he's not sure how to become the job he now holds.

"The big picture world hasn't changed. I've been in this business for years and years. I know the lingo, too. At the bank, there were lots of players, each with mastery of an important niche. Over the years, I learned how to talk to every one of those guys, how to get to the answers—you know the equity capital markets guy who says 'It's definitely going to fall within the range' and you learn to say 'Where will it trade?'" What Serruto didn't have was the lore of his new field, the analogies and famous deals everyone refers to. "I started out asking 'What do you mean?' but Eric was saying, 'What do you mean "What do you mean"?' so I stopped asking." Time solved that problem.

But Language from the Edge, which served Serruto well in keeping clients happy, isn't powerful enough for the world of traders. "These guys say stuff like 'That's right. It's going to be twenty-seven.' We were never as definite as that about anything. I was careful. Everything I said was conditional . . . not totally hedgy or elusive, like the guys we used to interview from law schools. But not like these guys either." The culture of his work is now more about statements than questions. He needs the boldness of authority, but he's more comfortable with the questions of exploration. He spent a decade in New York so he's comfortable interrupting, but interrupting to say "Okay, okay, can you walk me through that?" rather than "That's not going to happen" or "No, you'll like this better" or "That's wrong."

Serruto is in the middle of figuring out how to move from one world of work to another. He's not the new kid like Peter Smith. Like Judy Sedlar, he has a niche of expertise, but not one that has been of use so far. He needs to observe carefully the world of work around him, integrate what he can, and modify the rest to fit who he is. This is a process Harvard Business School professor Herminia Ibarra calls "negotiated adaptation."

It may work—or it may not. The office is small. There's no one that can help Serruto with the transition—Eric's in his office with the door shut, thinking. Serruto is expected to grow the business and make the most of what Eric is thinking about. He will have to adopt Language from the Center, the style of investor management, if he wants credibility among his peers. But he doesn't want to lose the sense of who he is and what he does well. His old style was part of his badge of experience, so he is more resistant to adaptation and change than were Sedlar or Smith. Mid-career and not exactly where he wants to be, Serruto may find that the transition is feasible but unappealing to him. Then again, if he can land a big account or sign up a major client, the power of reinforcement could turn the tide. Ultimately, he may end up being a financial adviser with a unique style, one that merges deference and swagger. But adopting a new role is hard work and mixing the deference and inquiry of the edge with the authority and directiveness of the center won't be easy. To begin with, before he can innovate, Serruto's got to take hold of the language of his new work, Language from the Center, and let go of what didn't happen.

SAME WORK, NEW EMPLOYER

> 1. Use Language from the Center for credibility. 2. Know your audience. 3. Cross-examine criticism.

Susan McCann trained as a journalist and began her career calling in stories on Los Angeles City Council meetings for 10 P.M. deadlines. She left that work to go to law school and worked for the next decade with a large telecommunications company. In 1990, she became general counsel for a start-up operation in cable broadcasting. When the partners decided their dream project was actually a nightmare, McCann's contract gave her the luxury of six months to choose a new job. She is presently general counsel for a national network of radio stations.

In one sense, McCann's work hasn't changed much in twenty years. She's had to learn new regulations and new names around the conference table. But speech style also figures into her transitions. "I'm still a general counsel so, in a sense, I haven't changed jobs. But this is different. And it's not different as much because of the corporate culture as because of the time curve I'm on right now. I've only been here a year. I am more judicious at this point, watching to see if I'm trusted yet and working to assess the level of sophistication of the organization. I am learning when people need a primer and when I can work in shorthand. I knew all that at Omnicable. And they knew me. I knew who to coddle and who I could talk to in bullet points." But like Serruto and the student teachers, McCann, an expert in her field, hasn't built up full credibility yet in this particular "classroom." She had to begin as something of an observer. But the time she had for this job search helped her do extensive homework on the company before her first day on the job. In particular, she figured out the glaring weaknesses of the previous general counsel and aimed her initial energy at that. Again, fixing an existing problem in a visible and innovative way builds power. And claiming authority in this area is expected and welcomed.

"Whomever I'm talking to, I choose my words carefully. That comes from my law school training and the luck of clerking with a judge who took it seriously. But I also mastered that talent calling in news stories and dictating them over the phone. I strive for an economy of words. I don't use colloquialisms, I try to be as clear as possible, and I don't take the floor and hold forth. I rarely swear—once in a while for effect or to channel the intensity out of a situation. I try not to talk over other people although when I need to take control—at a meeting or when someone is taking more than his share of the conversation—I will break in. I might ask, 'Does anyone have anything new to add?' [a nice blend of the center's interruptive strategy and the edge's use of a question]. I try to speak with assurance and to choose my words with precision. I do a good job because I know the business and I work hard at it, but I think my speech style *is* part of my authority . . . other people have told me this, too."

McCann's expertise and credibility may need time to build. In the meantime, she is making statements and contextualizing with expertise, not wrapping her points in caveats and disclaimers. In meetings, she prefaces her recommendations with an invitation: "If you wish, I can go into the details, but essentially what we should do is . . ." She does not say, "I'm new at this so . . ." or "Correct me if I'm way off base here."

Her speech strategies, combined with her overall experience, a first-rate assistant, and the power inherent in her position, have made McCann's transition a success. But remember the studies that show speakers who claim authority can inspire critical reactions? The authority of Language from the Center, when used by men and particularly when used by women, can provoke negative judgments. And so, about six months into the new job, McCann was invited to have lunch in the company club room with Louise Heath, a senior vice president. McCann assumed this was just part of the sociability of colleagues who both report directly to the company's CEO, but five minutes into the meal, her colleague explained a different motive:

> You know, I invited you to lunch because I need to give you some constructive feedback. I've wondered if I should say anything and I didn't really want to say anything. But I remember that I had these same thoughts about Martha before they let her go—afterward, I felt like I should have said something, like I'd missed a chance to be helpful. And there just isn't

105

a nice way to say this. You're a great lawyer and all that—I think Walter made a great hire. But there are a lot of people here who feel like you are authoritarian, abrupt, you know, rude. They feel you have no sense of humor. A few pleases and thank-you's would go a long way to making friends here. We *are* a southern company, you know.

McCann was astonished. She played for time and said, "Well, tell me about Martha." While she half listened to the sad tale of Martha, a marketing director who lasted only a year, McCann thought about what she'd heard. This senior VP was telling her that her speech style, something she viewed as a strength, was a weakness. Had she misread the company, misunderstood the language culture of the job, already made a pack of enemies? She thought about her career so far, her last job, her present boss. No, this didn't make sense.

In the end, McCann concluded that her colleague's objections were part of the price of Language from the Center. Knowing that authority and leadership can inspire negative reactions, she didn't do anything right away. "I knew I didn't have to take Louise's message as truth. I thought about the conversation, listened to myself a little, and after a while, maybe a week, I stopped in and chatted with my boss about how he thought things were going *in general*. I never asked him if he was dissatisfied with my style, just whether he thought I was getting the work done and establishing myself. He was very positive . . . in fact, I got a raise two or three weeks later. So I haven't made any particular adjustments—I was determined not to let criticism of a strength turn it into a weakness." McCann reconnected to a source of confidence, cross-examined the criticism, and decided not to pay any particular attention to this "disarming friend." She's still hoping someday to hear the complete Martha story.

McCann's new job requires careful observation of the way things are done in the new setting, a willingness to learn, and a prompt establishment of authority. But it also requires level-headed objectivity and a willingness to cross-examine the "please be nice" message that authority and power can elicit. Language from the Edge might seem safer, but Language from the Center builds credibility and gets work done. Claiming your expertise—with a sharp eye for what's really going on and a deaf ear for jealousy posing as free advice—is an important mid-career skill.

INTERNAL PROMOTION

> 1. Establish authority early. 2. Expect new power to change old friendships (change of power without change of place is the most difficult transition). 3. Abandon junior career skills in senior positions.

Melinda Dietz has worked her way up from an entry-level position in marketing at a flight training company and is the new vice president of Airflight's client management operation. Dietz is one of three vice presidents and one of twelve people who report to Airflight's president, Jeff Snyder. Snyder was Dietz's boss when she was a director and the two have gotten along well throughout the association. She knows and likes the other two VPs, both of whom have been helpful and supportive. She can sell her ideas to them and even to Snyder before she presents them in a meeting, so she feels secure about her ability to manage her group.

But Dietz noticed that the support staff "snapped to attention like I'm the enemy" when she walked through the work area. To complicate matters, several of her former colleagues didn't acknowledge her promotion. Tom, who has always been hardheaded and unwilling to listen to any side of a story but his own, gets into phone conversations with Dietz that seem like a threat to her new position.

Tom: You ought to be able to do something about this for me.

Melinda: You know I can't do that, Tom. Everybody had the same chance to put in for this and the decision's been made.

Tom: Come on, Mel, we go way back . . . you can get this for me if you want to.

Dietz feels like hanging up on the guy. She isn't sure how to establish authority with someone who insists they are buddies.

Dietz's problem is a common one when we try out new power in an old setting. Author Lorene Cary describes this problem in her memoir, *Black Ice*. A best friend challenges Cary's new position in the school's administration:

"I can't believe that you've let this vice-president crap go to your head . . . I really didn't think you'd take it this way." . . . I didn't want her to think I'd joined the establishment, but the truth was that, in a way, I had. I went back to my hot little den to lick my wounds and convince myself . . . that I'd found something better.

Any promotion affords a boost to confidence and an affirmation of talents. But internal promotions are the hardest to negotiate. When people who were formerly colleagues—people you shared a beach house with or bonded with by complaining about the previous VP—are subject to your new authority, power can prove elusive and bittersweet. A lateral move into a new firm would have been easier for Dietz.

So at the first meeting of all her divisions, Dietz chose Language from the Edge. She began by announcing, "I'm excited about this promotion but I'm new at it and I'm counting on all of you to help me make it a success." She built the meeting around a series of questions for division heads to respond to. She felt this inquiring approach from the edge was the key to her success with clients and she hoped to use it in her new position.

Team approaches work pretty well when a diverse group of people come together on a time-sensitive project. But the concept is not as successful if it's applied to the ongoing organization of a department or a division. Teams, after all, have captains, leaders, coaches, or someone who can cut the kid who never comes to practice. There's nothing stress-free about team dynamics. Competition for positions, accusations of favoritism, and internal politics are only occasionally broken with bursts of truly selfless teamwork in the heat of competitive play.

Like Serruto, Dietz has to let go, move on, and set aside one set of skills for another. Dietz's new job requires Language from the Center and a solid affect of authority. "People say they want a leader to be vulnerable just like them, but deep down they want to believe you have the skill to move and fix things they can't," says Hewlett-Packard's Cynthia Danaher. "And while anyone who starts something new is bound to feel some anxiety, you don't have to bare your soul." Team building within the division and collaborative listening may be the primary strategy on the way to promotion, but right now Dietz needs to set a direction for the division, delegate responsibility, and make clear to her people that she has a plan and the power to enact it. Dietz can ask questions and work collaboratively with the other VPs and her professional counterparts. She shouldn't lose her responsive tools. But she will have to accept the new mix of styles, the loss of friendships from her former position, and the new authority of Language from the Center. Such language can give you professional firepower, but you'll also have to take the heat.

THE RULES FOR JOB TRANSITION

1. Start on the edge: be a sponge.
2. Borrow authority from those you work for.

3. Build power with work that is visible, innovative, and solves an existing problem.
4. Look for a significant specialization or additional skill that will justify Language from the Center.
5. Move to the center: be a leader.
6. Know your audience *and* do your homework: ideas don't sell themselves.
7. Learn new language for new work.
8. Remember it's easier to claim new power or adopt a new speech style in a new setting.
9. When you achieve power, expect at least one friend to tell you "You've changed" or that you sound strident, officious, or stuck on yourself. Shake it off.

INSTANT AUTHORITY: ADD WATER AND MIX

In a country dedicated to athletics (or at least to the shirts and the shoes), sandlot baseball, pickup basketball, and the seasonal rotation of televised sports are familiar athletic territory. Sweep rowing, commonly called crew, is not. In a boat designed roughly along the same lines as a number two pencil, nine people strive to cover two thousand meters of water in less than six minutes. What looks smooth and glamorous in the bank commercials and at the Olympics is a sport of fierce competition and muscle-crushing exertion. The physiology of rowing places extraordinary demands on the body and generates mind-numbing pain. It is a given that a crew should neither be able to speak nor to move at the end of a race. And while every collegiate sport asks its participants to put in several hours of daily practice, crew demands an insane number of training hours when you figure the performance isn't a three-set match or eighteen holes or four periods: it's five minutes and fifty-four seconds—or less.

The boat comprises four pairs of port and starboard rowers. Heavyweight men's crews include eight rowers weighing about 200 pounds each. A lightweight rower averages 155 pounds, women, 130 pounds. Out on the water, overseeing what lightweight oarsman Jesse Elzinga calls "this band of ruffians," is the cox. The smallest of those in the boat, the cox never touches an oar. How does the little person manage all those big people? The cox, an unusual athlete by any standard, offers a lesson in establishing authority.

Now, the cox isn't just along for the ride. She is in charge of the equipment and she coordinates the launch. She knows the river, the conditions, and the details of the practice. She interprets the coach's plan for the day. And in a race, she's the only person in the boat who can see the finish line or observe the competition. Responsible for what happens on the water and for the safety of the boat and crew, she must motivate and correct the rowers' work in order to maximize their performance. She must choose and steer a course that makes the most of others' efforts. She can't win the race by her own efforts, but she can lose it by her own errors.

Psychologist, cheerleader, and the voice of authority in the boat, the cox, probably about five foot two and definitely only 120 pounds, must harness the power of eight oarsmen. Speech plays a role in her success or failure.

THE MOTIVATION OF A LEADER

It's the common assumption among rowers that coxes love to push people around. But when coxes themselves talk about their power, they talk about the power to help others succeed. Coxes share their coaches' and oarsmen's intense commitment to winning. Often accomplished athletes in other sports, they bring to the river all the competitiveness they used to display on a court, in a rink, or on the diamond. Robert Henry, a men's varsity lightweight cox, says, "My motive is for us all to do well." He pauses. He smiles with conviction. He adds, "To win."

And in this sport, no one can do well alone. Unlike basketball or baseball players, no oarsman can say "I had a great race" if the boat didn't win. So like all leaders, the cox wants success but she wants it for her entire group, not just for herself (she could, after all, row a single if she wanted singular glory).

The Expertise of a Leader

The cox studies the technical aspects of the race. She must also know something about the act of rowing. The best coxes have firsthand information about technique, mistakes, and how to correct them. She studies videos and listens to her own race tapes. Cox Nancy Poon says, "Even from the first day, I have to know one thing more than they do. Then I emphasize what I know. I talk to the coach or analyze the weather. I know the Boston side or the wind. I do my homework."

On the shore, the cox is in continual conversation with the coaches, borrowing both information and authority from them. She knows her oarsmen, too, knowing that some like to be hounded, others like to be praised. Where there is a problem, the cox must offer a solution. Julia Brookins, another experienced cox, says, "You can't be negative in a way that doesn't give a solution. Never leave a problem hanging out there." It's not useful to say "Two seat, you're early." The cox must know what will change the problem and be directive: "Two seat, square your blade." When a little person who never rows must establish authority among eight very big people who do all the work, knowledge helps.

The best coxes know one other thing: themselves. They work from within their own confidence, knowledge, and style. They don't copy other coxes or believe in scripts or simple routines. They capitalize on a chemistry they can create in a boat and they build success from that. This is the elusive piece that can't be taught: the personal modifications within the standard script.

THE STRATEGY OF A LEADER

On the water, the cox has one unusual advantage. She can see the finish line, the other boats, the upcoming bridge. She knows the future is not what lies before the rowers' eyes, but rather what sneaks up behind them. Jeff Lindy, author of the Ninthman Web site and also a varsity cox, stresses the importance of good information: "Without it, the crew starts snatching glances over their shoulders for the finish buoys and the cox becomes 120 pounds of useless ballast." Rob Henry says, "I want to paint a clear picture for my oarsmen so they know what's going on . . . and know that I know what's going on." This may mean concrete information about opponents, buoys, and bridges. It may also mean the shared vision of the whole race, the future.

THE SOUND OF LEADERSHIP

Are coxes perfect? Not always. Sometimes wisdom and vision come together; the rest of the time, they fake it. "I put on the air of being infallible," says Henry.

"It's easy to be cast as the bitchy overseer," says Irene Hahn, an experienced cox. "My goal is to make it as easy as possible for the rowers to think only about rowing. If you establish authority from the beginning, if your oarsmen trust you, they will perform."

Mistakes happen. A stroke is lost or a call is questioned. The best response, according to Henry, is to acknowledge it and put it behind you: "Okay, I see that. Now if you do your job, I will do my job. Let's go." When a cox needs correction from the lead oarsman (the stroke), those conversations are held with the microphone off.

Hahn believes that the authority of the cox liberates the oarsmen from concern. Tone of voice and speech style are critical in accomplishing this: "You have to sound like you know what you're doing even if you don't . . . it is incredibly frustrating for an oarsman to have a tentative person in the stern who can't bring out the best in them." Lindy concurs: "Coxswains must speak with an absolute tone of certainty." Brookins lays out the wrong way: "No one will row for a cox who says 'Come on, guys' in a whiny little voice." Poon recommends, "End every sentence with a period, never a question mark." In a race, anger, indecision, and impatience all sound like a cox with no faith in the crew.

Coxes walk with confidence as well as talk with confidence. There's a bit of cockiness involved, no doubt. But outright arrogance is the right strategy only once in a while. You need absolute control of the timing. Arrogant posturing can demoralize or embarrass oarsmen, motivate the opponent, and lose a race. "See you later, assholes" works best when your bow is already over the finish line.

Do all coxes sound the same? No. Each one has a style, a blend of encouragement, information, and highly charged screaming. Some swear ("Mostly I cuss a lot" was the self-proclaimed secret of the 1968 U.S. Olympic cox). Others invoke the generals of Roman imperialism, the captivity in Babylon ("I want to hear the lamentations of their women"), or the beaches of Operation Overlord. Some use names; most use seat numbers. But they all agree that their style is a result of what works for their oarsmen. They all sound confident and in control. And in a race, the very best sound intensely involved, positive, and excited. "You can be the best cox at correcting a crew and you can be the best at steering a boat, but you won't cox the varsity unless you can bring the energy of excitement into the boat," says oarsman David Weiss.

THE COST OF LEADERSHIP

Is this fun? Maybe. Is it easy? No. Coxes take a lot of criticism and almost all the blame when a boat loses a race. The cox, like any leader, cannot win the battle but he can most assuredly lose the war. The internal competition within his "organization" is tricky, too. As Hahn says, "Seat races [the competition for individual places in a varsity boat] are a source of unending misery. Once the lineups are established, the first boat is full of people who think this has always been their due. The second boat is full of malcontents who think they were cheated out of a place in the first boat." The cox has to think about her own boat and her individual oarsmen in crafting the best motivation and the right strategy. And she has to know that when things go wrong, it will be her fault first, then the coaches', then the weather . . . and maybe then the rowers'. In the end, the victories are celebrated and the problems need to be "left on the water."*

LEARNING FROM THE COX

In your own work, be a good cox.

1. Enjoy the power of your role but use it for the good of the whole boat.
2. Do your homework. Use every resource available to create expertise, the basis of authority.
3. Borrow authority from your coach or any other leader who will endorse you and your ideas.
4. Take input and give praise in public. Give and take criticism in private. Put it all to the same use: your pride in your group's achievement. Leave the small slights and daily dustups of every job "on the water"—no grudges, revenge, or deep victories.
5. Know your people. You can't motivate everyone in the same way.
6. Strive for trust. Have a plan, seek endorsement from above (the coach) and below (the oarsmen). Communicate your information and vision. Expect flak.

*With thanks to Julia Brookins, Jesse Elzinga, Irene Hahn, Robert Henry, Jeff Lindy, Nancy Poon, and David Weiss for their words, insight, and reflections.

7. You can call your style "team management" if you want, but remember that teams are full of internal politics, turf wars, competitiveness, and resentment. Teams need a captain, a leader, or a cox. They want their leader to be wise, fair, and enthusiastic.

8. Speak with confidence and encouragement. Be assured, positive, and knowledgeable (and only genuinely cocky at the finish line).

CHAPTER SIX
ELECTRONIC
COMMUNICATION

Your call will be answered in the order in which it was received.

In *The Paper*, Michael Keaton wants to avoid a phone call from his boss. But she's found him from her car phone and she's about to tell him something he doesn't want to hear. If only he didn't have to talk to her! Keaton grabs a sheet of paper off his desk and crumples it over the mouthpiece of the phone. "Alicia . . . Alicia . . . there's a lot of static," he says. "I'm losing you. Are you in the tunnel?"

As his boss struggles to be heard, Keaton continues to crinkle the paper. The audience can hear her barking commands with perfect clarity. But Keaton pursues the ploy: "I can't . . . we can't . . . we can't hear you . . . we'll see you when you get in, okay?" He puts down the receiver. "I love car phones." He smiles. Ah—modern technology. It's teaching us all sorts of new tricks.

Business bristles with new communication gadgets, tools we have adopted with almost universal enthusiasm. Got a cell phone? Got a laptop? Got instant messaging? The guy in the next cube has a Blackberry and swears it's changed his life. He can no more explain the mechanism than he can the principle that made possible his flight from Cleveland. But he's figured out three of the functions and can justify the expense best by telling you he can't live without it. Why are you still in the Dark Ages?

The pressure to own these things derives from a curious assumption: habits can be bought. We believe that what we own can change who we are. And we excuse what we don't do by what we don't have. If I had a nice desk, I'd write a novel. If I had my own office, I'd get more done. The hundreds of thousands of dust-covered NordicTracks, free weights, and rowing machines in the basements of America were purchased with the same vision: if I had a machine, I'd exercise. And we buy a Palm Pilot to make us more organized, a laptop so we'll get those reports done on time, e-mail so the office will work like a team. Maybe it will happen. Maybe it won't.

Although we are quick to purchase and endorse all these new work tools, we are slow to read the instruction manual. Didn't every eighties office have its undisturbed row of stout gray DOS boxes? Even with instruction, the learning curve can be steep and there's lots of language to master. Tech support personnel deal every day with the guy who can't open his e-mail attachments. Or the woman whose pc won't respond to the "right-click your mouse" command the IT staffer offers over the phone. When the staffer heads upstairs to give hands-on help, he finds a screen with eight copies of the sentence "Click your mouse" blinking on it. Seems she thought he said, "Write 'Click your mouse.'" Finally, while IT will teach you the important functions and uses of your gizmo, they don't have much to say about the wise use of the product. Don't eat it or use it in the bathtub. Okay . . . anything else?

Comfortable already with typewriters, copiers, and computers, we don't think much about the latest electronic additions to the office. Every new thing must be a better thing. But if you've ever inadvertently left a page in the copier, you know that electronic communication isn't fully charted territory. It's not the same writing, typing, and talking we've always done. This is why e-mail is turning out to be a bit of a nightmare.

In most situations, face-to-face communication is the ideal. The strength of this format sends presidents around the world, peace negotiators to dangerous sites, and business people to Frankfurt (sometimes twice in one week). Since words produce something only approximately like what we mean, meeting face-to-face offers the best chance of clear communication. When we see confusion on the listener's face, we can repeat, modify, or even withdraw our message. When we see happy acceptance, we can cut out the apologetic explanation. I am always stunned by how easily facial expressions and silent cues confuse (and correct) a student's answers in class. Cornered by a question like "Damon, were the Puritans a tolerant community?" the hapless student knows to start talking. He looks for answers in the air: "Yes . . . Yes . . . [buying time] in many ways, I mean kind of . . . they came here for religious freedom." The rest of the class shifts in their seats and he sees two hands in front of him go up with the confidence of contradiction. I tilt my head and look confused. "But not really," he adds. The hands go down. "I think they wanted freedom for themselves when they came here." Now I'm nodding and looking directly at him. "But once they got here . . . uhhh . . . I don't think they were very tolerant of others . . . right?" I'm smiling. Life is good. Clear communication and understanding has the best chance when speakers sit at the same table or meet in the same room. Spoken language involves an enormous array of subtle elements—pitch and inflection, the surround of body language, the context and conventions of a specific group of speakers. These features are essential parts of meaning.

Written language is tame by comparison. Without pitch and pause, gesture and facial expression, standard written English tries to keep misunderstanding under control. Full sentences, correct spelling, clear pronoun reference, and properly placed modifiers aim at clarity. Reading transcripts of the Microsoft testimony or the Clinton impeachment hearings makes clear how fragmented conversation is, how many "rules" we break with every breath, and how amazing is the operation of understanding. Voice mail messages, e-mail, and phone work are affected by the loss of the features of face-to-face conversation (e-mailers sometimes add a smile or a <groan> to replicate speech); these communications survive without the rules and regulations of standard written English and with only some of the features that assist face-to-face verbal exchanges.

Lawrence Lessig, a Harvard Law School professor, noted in a recent *New York Times* article: "E-mail is perhaps the most contextually sensitive piece of writing that we have, and culturally we're going through this stage where we don't understand how to read it." Lack of context can make a message seem abrupt or random, rude or arrogant. Lessig points out that unless we can learn to manage the technology, we will lose the advantages of quick and spontaneous communication. But the new communication tools don't come with a full set of instructions partly because the rules are still evolving. These forms of communication seem familiar and benign but the differences in each of them mean you should proceed with caution.

E-MAIL

E-mail borrows the latitude of speech communication in a presentation that seems like writing. Note the memo header, however. This is not a standard business letter. The rules of standard written English don't apply. Fragments are the preferred material of most messages and without "include message in reply" many responses seem like non sequiturs.

> "That's fine. I'll see you there."
> "But didn't we already send this to STL?"
> "Thanks, you're right, it wasn't a problem."
> "Hope this is helpful."

If your correspondent makes functional use of the "Re:" or "Subject" line—typing "I was wondering" or "Thanks for the P/E numbers"—the message itself may just barely make sense:

>   . . . if you'd heard from KC about the 16th.
>   . . . but where's the chart?

The writer has your text in front of her and offers what is only half a conversation. It's easy to forget the question you sent two days ago.

Speed rules. Speed of delivery, coupled with speed of composition, can make e-mail absolutely cryptic or entirely unreadable. College students, who check their e-mail about two thousand times a day, treasure this convention. In the first place, correction was a huge inconvenience on early, key-driven programs. No one cared about typos. The tolerance for error, even with software that includes a spell-checker, remains high. As long as typos don't interfere with understanding, errors don't mean ignorance, only haste. E-mail is meant to be spontaneous and informal. It's great for confirming a plan or asking a quick question. It retains the spirit of the phone message or the pink memo slip, rather than the interoffice memo or the short letter.

>   "Can we reschedule? I'm swamped."
>   "Jack finally called. Call me."

Further evidence of the premium put on speed, rather than careful crafting, is e-mail's own vocabulary of acronyms: BTW (by the way), IMHO (in my humble opinion), LOL (laughing out loud), FWIW (for what it's worth).

E-mail, with the casualness and plasticity of speech but without the inflections or context, still looks like written communication sitting there on the screen. It can feel like a letter when the content is negative. Sarcasm, in particular, gets lost. The keyboard characters called emoticons ;-(:-p aren't quite enough to soften a critical, negative, or unwelcome message. If I write:

"Can we reschedule? I'm swamped," and you write: "Call me when you aren't so busy," your response sounds cold and judgmental. If you type: "Call me when you aren't so busy ☺," your message seems more like "I understand. You must be working hard. I'm happy to meet with you at another time (and when we do meet, I will be glad to see you)." But that's a heavy burden to put on a smiley face; there is plenty of potential in e-mail for confusion, offense, and misunderstanding.

HINTS FOR SURVIVING E-MAIL COMMUNICATION

E-mail is brief and speedy, like a voice mail message, but it's a tricky little patch of the communication field. There are a few mines out there, some barbed wire, and spots where misunderstanding is going to happen. Know your company policies on electronic communication. Check to see if e-mails and Internet addresses are stored and reviewed. And proofread for both typos and tone.

FOR SENDING

1. Keep it short. Don't ask anyone to read more than a screenful of anything. If you have that much to say, phone, fax, write—or send them a valentine. A really long message may be skimmed or closed to be read later (also known as never). People expect to run through their e-mail like a bowl of pistachio nuts. And you know what happens to the ones that are hard to open.

2. Don't type messages in upper-case letters. It reads as though you are shouting. Standard upper and lower cases are fine and, if you're feeling poetic and a bit like e. e. cummings, you can use all lower case. But lay off the caps lock.

3. Do not deal with difficult, highly personal, or sensitive material in an e-mail message. Do not take someone off a project, present a complicated proposal or request, or de-

cline an important offer in this format. There's too much potential for misunderstanding. If this is an important message, it's important enough to merit a face-to-face meeting or a phone call.

4. Try to limit the number of important questions asked or issues presented. Recipients usually reply to the last thing you say and they never scroll back or remember your early questions. Ask or tell the most important thing last.

5. Use that forward function sparingly. Both Morgan Stanley Dean Witter and Citigroup settled lawsuits brought over offensive jokes forwarded on the company's internal e-mail system. The guy who forwards jokes is asking for trouble—and willing to look like he doesn't have much work to do. Forwarding another's message is sort of like wearing a body mike; you are passing along material without the author's permission. Consider summarizing or sending a section of the message by cut-and-paste.

6. Think before e-mailing an important document as an attachment. Incompatible software can leave your document unread and people in a hurry or worried about viruses don't open attachments.

7. Borrow from standard letter conventions. A good "cc" still makes things happen. A salutation—"Great to hear from you" or "Thanks for the note"—cushions what follows; messages that dive right into the topic sound rude and sometimes angry. Include your name and contact information in business e-mail.

8. Capture the address from any mail you receive. Consider printing out your address book occasionally. Some crashes and viruses erase saved name and address information.

9. Do not write anything in e-mail that you wouldn't be willing to see on a billboard by the entrance ramp to I-95 with your name attached to it. With just a little innocent and not-so-innocent forwarding, this could happen. E-mail is not private.

10. E-mail works best where one response (or no response) is required. E-mail to schedule a meeting with multiple op-

tions (even when both parties want to meet) can be frustrating:

> Monday: "When do you want to do this?"
> Tuesday: "How about Wednesday at 10?"
> Wednesday: "I'm booked today but I can do Friday at 10."
> Thursday: "I'm out of town tomorrow."
> Friday: "I guess next week makes more sense. How about Monday at 10?"

The colossal delay here only makes sense if someone is deliberately stalling—and most people are savvy to that ploy. Pick up the phone.

11. Figure out who likes versus who rarely checks e-mail; you can usually tell who's a novice from the format of their messages. Plan your communications accordingly. If your recipient has her assistant print out e-mail for her to read, send faxes instead.

12. Avoid the exchange of worthless information that e-mail allows. If the idea is thirty seconds old, it's probably too hot to pass along. Reflect, let things cool, then share.

13. If you require an immediate response, consider a phone call *and* an e-mail. Not answering e-mail is vastly more common than not returning phone calls . . . although the volume of these communications means not answering either is more common than it was in the past.

14. Don't answer your e-mail while you're on the phone. We can tell.

FOR REPLYING

1. Let clients and coworkers know if you check your e-mail only rarely. If you don't check regularly, you should give up the account. If it's part of the office system, however, you're just going to have to adjust. You don't have to

send but you will have to receive. Remember, out of the loop can be out of a job.

2. Senders can be sure their message is sent, but not that the right jonathan smith is at *jsmith@aol.com*. We all get those .net, .com, .org addresses confused. Reply promptly, even if just to say "I don't know but I'll look into it."

3. Reply to all the queries within the message, not just to the last question asked.

4. The Microsoft trial suggests that moderation is protection. Try to retain spontaneity but rein in your tone. Talk about competing, not murdering. Ask for specific performance numbers, not for heads on platters. Respect your competitors; avoid war words.

5. Think twice before you hit Send. Ask a colleague or save as a draft and consider. Imagine a reader who's not your best friend when you proofread your reply. Speed is great, but a dismissive, can't-be-bothered response won't help you the next time you meet this correspondent. If you "fire off" responses, you will get burned.

6. Alan receives a reprimand from his boss, forwards it to his partner with "Can you believe this garbage?" His partner adds "What a jerk!!" and hits Send and "all recipients"—and both Alan and his boss receive the three messages. Be especially careful with the "Reply to all recipients" option for messages, particularly messages that are already responses or are "forwards" to you. It's easy to forget what's in those earlier messages hidden below the screen. And it's easy to skip rereading who the original recipients were.

7. Respond promptly.

    Monday: "Can you do lunch tomorrow?"
    Tuesday at 2 P.M.: "Oh wow, sorry—I just got your message. Maybe another time."

    Messages sent after a suggested meeting time seem like a deliberate strategy to avoid the contact.

8. Joining listservers can be useful and interesting but you need

125

to know that all listservers go through the same life cycle. Weigh what you're learning against the time it takes to open twenty messages a day (especially when the first one's from Bob and the next nineteen say "Right on, Bob!").

9. Reply with targeted precision. Don't choose "Reply to all recipients" if you've received a listserver message and want to comment directly to the sender. No one—except Bob—wants to read a long list of messages that all say "Bob, you're right on with that one!" Direct those hearty congratulations to Bob, not to the whole list.

10. Watch out for "Lost in Headerland." An e-mail group that circulates information entirely by Reply is tricky territory. A key member of an important subcommittee was "blacked out" when, about a week into the project, a colleague chose to delete her name from the subcommittee's e-mail header of recipients. Messages continued to be exchanged through "Reply." No one else in the group ever checked or noticed who was (or wasn't) in the header. The deleted person wondered why the committee wasn't getting much done, but assumed everyone was just busy with other work. The rest of this story is ugly.

11. E-mail can be written by someone other than the header name on the message; not all e-mail is "real."

FINAL THOUGHTS

While speed and spontaneity are the strengths of e-mail, they are also its nemeses. We've all hit Send and regretted it. But you can't take that message out of the letterbox and tear it up. Impulsiveness needs to be moderated. Some thoughts are unguarded and better kept to ourselves; others are "rough drafts" that lack necessary reflection. Sharing momentary reactions that have to be corrected (or withdrawn) later is embarrassing. Sharing useless speculations and undeveloped ideas wastes other people's time. Don't let the speed of e-mail seduce you.

And don't count on e-mail for much in the interpersonal department. In business, it's a superior tool for contacting people with updates and brief messages. It works especially well for positive messages. It can keep the ball rolling, but it's about as rich and subtle as a Post-it note. If complicated issues or negotiations need to happen, do them face-to-face. Praise works best in person or with voice mail's nuances of emotion. If one-sided, traceable, or complex declarations need to be made, draft a letter. And if you receive e-mail that is troubling or inappropriate, print, save, and talk to your boss about it.

Voice Mail

Alexander Graham Bell began designing communication devices for the deaf. He conceived of the telephone as a means of conversation for people separated by one or two rooms. He did not, at first, see it as a way to talk to Katmandu. But telephone technology has been one of the most significant innovations in this century: the phone, the modem, the conference call, the fax, and Internet access have remade the world of work. But we are all learning how to use the phone differently. It isn't often about one-to-one communication anymore. "Your call is important to us. Please stay on the line for the next available operator"—if my call were important, a human being would answer it. "I'm not available to take your call"—kind of obvious. Phone connection these days means listening to repeated assurances and insincere apologies, staying focused for complicated options, and crafting messages that will prompt a response. Before you can get anywhere, you will have to spell Valdepenas-Orenstein into the company directory (you can get subversive and hit 0, hoping for a human being by default) and press 1 to hear about those other options. You will inevitably find your target away from his desk. If you leave a message, you'll get ambushed by the limit tone. You'll recite your phone number much too fast. When he calls back, you'll be away from your desk. And he'll recite his phone number much too fast.

A message like the following is a waste of electronic memory:

"Hi, Andrew. This is Stacey. Give me a call at 212-555-1214."
A message needs to move things along in some way, setting a
planned meeting and asking for confirmation or suggesting a
window for connection: "I need to know by five if I'm going to
include this in the next order" or "I'll be in the office first thing
tomorrow if you have questions." You might borrow the journalist's ploy and declare an immediate deadline.

Your own voice message doesn't have to be an encyclopedia
of information, however, since most of us have been leaving
messages now for twenty years. "I'm not at my desk" is pretty
obvious. "I'm either in a meeting or on the phone." Actually,
we don't care. Make sure the caller knows they've reached the
right party and, when relevant, any special constraints on
when the caller might hear back from you ("I'm out of the office today but . . ." or "I'm on vacation until the twenty-third
but my assistant, Aaron, at extension 1214 . . .").

Dante's Hell reflected the world of fourteenth-century Flo-

rence. If Hell is subject to updates, then sinners can expect to spend eternity on hold, listening to Vivaldi's *The Four Seasons* or NewsRadio, with periodic informational advertisements and insincere reassurances that their call really matters.

HINTS FOR SURVIVING VOICE MAIL COMMUNICATION

Your message:

1. Be brief. It is not necessary to say, "I can't answer the phone right now."
2. Sound welcoming. Plan and practice a message that is friendly, informative, and concise: "This is Lois Kunian. Kindly leave a message and your call will be returned." Smile while recording.
3. If possible, suggest a time when a caller might reach you directly.
4. Update your message daily (only if you update religiously). Listen to your own message periodically to be sure it's current and useful.
5. Less is more.

Leaving messages:

1. Listening to and leaving messages needs to take into account the elements lost without face-to-face communication. You can try to include the appropriate tones and pauses in your message, but remember you are talking without feedback. If your message is sensitive or your recipient important, play back your message and rerecord for the best effect.
2. Plan your message before you dial.
3. If you connect to a company directory message, listen to the complete instructions. Every system is different and the role of the # key is only revealed at the end!

4. Give your name and phone number at the beginning of the message. Include your area code (it's probably a new one). Repeat your number again at the end of the message, dictating it as though the other person is writing it down. She is.

5. Be brief but focus on leaving a message that advances the project or problem you are calling about. Establish a back-up plan for connecting (". . . or I will try you again at nine tomorrow"). Include a motivation for returning the call and some deadline or time constraint: "Hi, Andrew. It's Stacey at 212-555-1214. We need to talk about the INC order. I have questions about the color, the trim, and the delivery date. Call me tomorrow between eight and ten if you can—or call me today and leave a message about when you're available. I'm at 212-555-1214. Thanks. I think we can write this up as soon as these last three details get settled."

6. Know regional preferences. New Yorkers don't return voice mail as often as Midwesterners. Think about the local style.

7. Be careful about those "message in the future" options. If you leave one for your boss to be delivered at 8 P.M. and then go home at 7 P.M., can you guarantee that she won't call you in between?

GETTING THROUGH

A few thoughts on strategies for getting to a real person:

1. Hit 0 if you're pressed for time and get a multilayered menu. Make friends with 0.

2. Ask for a time when you can call back and reach the party directly.

3. Ask for an e-mail address and leave your own in your message.

4. Send a fax with your questions and follow up with a call.

5. If you're languishing on hold, try again and begin your request with "I won't be able to hold right now, so what's the best way to contact . . ." If you wait to explain your time limitation until the end of your request, you'll be on hold before you can explain.

6. Do some homework. Look up the target on the Internet and try to find a name, direct line, or extension that circumvents the main directory or departmental voice messaging system.

7. Prepare a short version of your question for the layers of transfer you'll have to go through before you connect. "I'm calling with a customer service issue" or "I need to speak to investor relations" might be a good start; you can give more information as you pass each hurdle on the way to the right person.

8. Leave highly specific messages. Think like your client— what do they need that you can provide? Put that in your message.

9. Leave no more than two voice messages for a specific individual. More feels like harassment. If you get no response, try a different individual, a different strategy—or try to make friends with 0: "Gee, I've been trying to get through to Roger Morales for several days and I'm wondering if he's out of town?" You might be able to win the sympathy of the main receptionist and this person might have a suggestion about how to get connected.

Interesting fact: companies that sell voice messaging equipment use real operators to answer calls.

OTHER PHONE WORK

Conference calls create meetings without travel. For the convenience of speaking to someone thousands of miles away, you sacrifice the visual cues. But you're still rowing with one oar and it takes planning and attention to keep on course.

Conference calls have their own etiquette. Each person on the call should introduce him/herself. No speaker should ask a question that is entirely self-serving. No speaker should use the end of the call to ask Jack to call them later or Beth to send them the EMG report. Don't plan to continue the call with one other person after the group hangs up, either. Others may be still on the call while you're doing this private postmortem. Call your colleague back if you want to dissect the conversation. And don't assume that conference calls will provide the same energy and involvement that a meeting would create. Most conference call participants have their phone on mute and are playing solitaire, leafing through their "to do" pile, or organizing their rubberband collection.

Beware of technological miscues. International connections can create one-second delays in a speaker's response. Each time you ask a question and wait just a little bit longer than usual for the answer, you wonder if the whole deal has cratered. You're surprised to hear "That sounds fine" after the long pause.

Video-conferencing tries to make up for the losses and keep everyone on task. If the technology is good, things go well. If the technology is poor, you will feel like you're watching a cheaply dubbed remake of *Godzilla*. International communication, in particular, suffers with the loss of face-to-face.

PORTABLE PHONES

A cell phone and a latte are part of today's business uniform. Car phones and beepers are part of the landscape. The phenomenon is spreading like mold on cheese. There are several sociology dissertations to be written about it all. The cell phone has been a status symbol for nearly a decade, for business people, drug dealers, and even for high school students who like to convey the message "I'm doing this right now but I have much more interesting things going on in my life." Now it's a matter of how and where you take your call that separates the dolts from the more delicate. Restaurants, theaters, churches, synagogues, classrooms, and private parties are not the ideal places to receive any kind of paging. And if you must let the world track you down, then excuse yourself from this more public setting and take your call in the hall. The details of the GM contract, the state of the CEO's health, and the latest development in the Cohen divorce all need to be protected. Since we talk on the phone in a louder voice than we use in a waiting room, street conversation, or walking around a mall, the most considerate portable phone callers stand still, whisper, and get out of the way.

Where the power balance is tipped against you, the cell phone/car phone call is going to seem like a slight. Don't make phone calls involving important negotiations or delicate interpersonal matters from a cell phone. You're likely to be cut off at the crucial moment.

About Faxes

As with cell phones, fax messaging raises important confidentiality issues. Faxes sometimes sit for hours on tables, in open mailboxes, or in the fax machine itself. Important medical information or highly confidential material should not be sent by fax without research about where the receiving machine is and who has access to it. Identifying information on cover sheets should include a disclaimer about misdirected faxes and a number to call to alert the sender of an error. Senders should check to be sure that faxes were received (machines are sometimes out of paper).

Hints for surviving phone communication

1. If you are screening your calls, don't pick up in the middle of a caller's message. Call back a few minutes later.
2. If a caller asks for you, don't ask, "Who's calling?" before you acknowledge that "This is Sarah McGinty." Be brave. If it's someone you don't want to talk to, you can deal

with that. And if it's someone you do want to talk to, and you've dodged the first query, you look evasive and shifty.

3. If you have call waiting, pick up only if the person with whom you are speaking suggests you take the other call. If there's an impending emergency, explain this to the caller at the beginning of the conversation: "I'd love to talk but I'm waiting for the start of a conference call; will you excuse me if I have to hop off?"

4. If you need to manipulate all this stuff just for the fun of it, answer the phone and say "Wait a second; I'll dump this other guy." Cheap flattery.

When Oliver North's e-mails were subpoenaed in the Iran-contra investigation, no one paid a lot of attention. When Bill Gates had to account for his own intracompany e-mails—answering "I don't remember" and "I don't know" to many of counsel's questions—it was already a different world. Like any other revolutionizing change in society, electronic communication arrived without protocols and with instruction manuals short on the details for wise and careful use. Time will supply what's missing. And the rules and conventions will change. President Clinton's administration was content to leave the Internet unregulated. But regulation may be needed. The courts are beginning to identify some of the thornier bits of the technology. The University of Michigan dealt with a student whose e-mails were judged to be threatening to another student. Several companies have fired employees for on-the-job misuse of the Internet; others have been sued in turn by their employees for allowing inappropriate messages to appear on the company system. Privacy rights complicate the monitoring of e-mail on company servers. Amazon.com, the online bookseller, noted in its company policy: "Quite simply put, there are some communications that should not be expressed in written form." So while all this sorts itself out, be conservative to survive.

ELECTRONIC DELEGATES

When would you be willing to let a colleague tell your boss you're taking Friday off? Maybe if you and your boss get on well and your colleague is your best pal in the world. Otherwise, you're more than likely to want to handle that transaction yourself. If you think of your e-mail, your cell phone, and your fax machine as delegates, machines willing to help you out but unlikely to add the spin of sympathy that your friend would provide, you'll call on these delegates with some caution. E-mail may feel like a conversation, but it works best for happy conversations. Voice messaging may seem like a phone call, but without the listener, you're talking in the dark. All these communication modes have borrowed conventions from speech and from writing but none offers the full features of speech. As novelist Richard Powers writes, "There would *be* no translation were it not for the fact there is *only* translation." All talk is translation. Your machines will work for you, if you recognize the limits of your delegates.

ONE FURTHER WORD ABOUT JOKES

Jokes are fun. Is it really necessary to put a ban on laughs? Here's a little scenario you may have already experienced: You open your listserver and find a message full of tasteless and offensive jokes. You look to see who sent them and then you pray for his skin. Three innocuous messages later, the same sender has written a pathetic, groveling apology about how incredibly inappropriate the sending was. The next eighty-four messages are full of shock and outrage. (The shock and outrage are supported by reference to individual jokes that appeared well below the first screen, where you stopped reading.) The next seven messages demand the sender's resignation from the listserver. On the following day, fifteen messages point out that tolerance is a virtue, that mistakes are often honestly made, that jokes of this type are not to be condoned or allowed on the listserver but that a recipe of

135

forgiveness, serenity, and First Amendment protections mean that we all need to lighten up and move on. One more outraged message will appear about two days later from someone whose server was down for forty-eight hours and then it will be over. Whether it's ever over for the guy who made the mistake, I can't say. Don't let this guy be you.

BACKSTAGE GLIMPSES

In March 1999, Amazon.com circulated a memo reminding employees that "there are some communications that should not be expressed in written form." The memo was at least in part inspired by the evidential use of corporate e-mail in the *United States v. Microsoft* trial. And while e-mail has become a convenient and—for some—indispensable way of doing business in the United States, the rules for its use are still evolving. If you use e-mail primarily for personal communications, you have probably experienced at least one e-mail horror story or instance of "flaming."

The Presentation of Self in Everyday Life, Erving Goffman's 1956 classic study of social psychology, predates Bitnet, the Internet, and e-mail. But Goffman's central metaphor, drawn from theater imagery, offers a useful framing for the dustups of electronic communication. Goffman views our human interactions as parts we perform for the "audience" of those around us, chosen from our repertoire according to the showing we wish to make. We offer our performance in what Goffman calls a front region. When we share a role with other people, we share a set of conventions that make us part of a team of performers. When we write an e-mail, then, we communicate within the context of one of our teams, speaking and acting according to our understanding of how managers, teachers, or consumers sound.

Backstage, however, the manner and appearance of the front

are dropped. The stockroom, for example, offers behavior not meant to be seen on the sales floor; the family table reveals manners never in evidence with guests; the waitstaff is transformed every time they pass through the kitchen door to the dining room. Bill Watterson's comic drawings of the life of Calvin and Hobbes occasionally depicted this backstage world. Calvin finds himself on an alien planet with disgusting monsters (all drinking coffee and smoking cigarettes). His inadvertent detour into the Teachers' Room at school is a visit to something very much like another planet where, without the monitoring audience of children, one might hear kids called "apprentice human beings" or assignments called "another fifty goddamn essays to correct."

The speed of e-mail has given the medium something of the feel of relaxed chatter. Typos and fragments are tolerated. Quick, brief responses are prized. Originating in military communication and systems organized within companies and on campuses, e-mail has the informality of "backstage" talk among a team, the spirit of messages among people with a shared vision—students, salesmen, military personnel—all talking just to each other. Most of us, in fact, began e-mailing among a fairly coherent group or team, a listserver of students, a group of faculty, a set of friends and family, or the employees of one department, business, or company.

The habit of forwarding messages and the proliferation of listservers, however, has broadened and diversified the audience of our performances. Those who began e-mailing among friends find the broader audience not as friendly. Those who began in their work setting are now working company to company, vendor to client, individual to professional group. Forwarded messages meet audiences they were never intended for, and the question of audience can get confusing.

When e-mail causes problems, it is often because the curtain has been drawn back and some accepted shorthand of thinking, some backstage lingo, has been revealed. The student says, "I can't stand old lady Bennett," the salesman says, "Let's screw the competition," the teacher calls the principal "an avenging bozo," the department manager says, "we need to light a fire under those guys in fulfillment." We all say such things as part of our backstage lives. Bill Gates and his team at Microsoft certainly did. We say them because we are all too human. And we say them as a means of connection through shared feelings. Bad-mouthing those who aren't around to hear us—"derogation of the absent"—is in part how a team or group maintains its morale. Like the pregame trash-talking of the athletes' locker room, these sentiments create bonds. Our backroom and backstage talk sounds like fighting words. Fortunately, we usually "meet under a temporary truce, a working consensus, in order to get business done." We don't often take the council of war onto the stage. E-mail, unfortunately, can take it there for us. Statements created in the spirit of backstage—the stockroom, the water cooler, the privacy of friendly banter—suddenly show up for all the world to see.

We are already seeing the conventions of e-mail drifting toward those of formal communication, where the "front" is maintained and backstage chatter is forbidden. Amazon.com suggests this in its internal memo, acknowledging the humanness of backstage banter while urging employees to recognize that such communications "should not be expressed in written form." Companies like CSFirst Boston and Morgan Stanley Dean Witter periodically remind employees that electronic communication may be subject to management storage and review. Other companies urge employees to add the protocols of formal business letters to e-mail communications or require disclaimers about the use of e-mail content. Until the full formality of the stage or public forum takes over e-mail, it will continue to embody both the pleasure of spontaneous and informal communication and the danger of accidental glimpses into the backstage words of our work.

CHAPTER SEVEN
A TRIP TO MARS AND VENUS

"A woman without her man is nothing."
"A woman: without her, man is nothing."

In 1999 United States trade representative Charlene Barshefsky explained in a Senate hearing why World Trade Organization negotiations between China and the United States had suddenly stalled. Barshefsky said: "Men never ask for directions, and we mistakenly bombed the Chinese Embassy in Belgrade. . . . That really chilled relations for almost five months." Barshefsky captured a complicated situation with an easy generalization: men are one kind of animal and women are another. Distribution of muscle mass, blood absorption of alcohol, average height, reproductive function: human biology is a good place to look for differences. But differences in how men and women act, think, and talk don't follow from the biology. These differences are more alive in cartoons, jokes, and stereotypes than in research, observation, and fact.

Nevertheless, the study of language in daily interactions—the discipline called sociolinguistics—has been, from the beginning, entwined with the study of gender. Established only in this century, sociolinguistics blossomed in the late 1960s and early 1970s, a time when political activism in the United States began to address important questions of equality and civil rights. Included among the earliest studies in the field was the topic of "sexism and language," shared ground for gender scholars and linguists. Long-standing grammatical conventions like the generic use of masculine pronouns ("Each of us has his hat"), the distinction of male and female practitioners of a trade or profession (actor/actress, author/authoress), and the connotative divergence of some of these pairs ("He's a master" and "She's a mistress," for example) gave academics and social commentators plenty to think and write about. The interest in women's issues and feminism that spawned the Equal Rights Amendment made the study of "sexism" in language a hot topic. Political correctness was born.

In 1973 University of California at Berkeley linguist Robin Lakoff published an essay entitled "Language and Woman's Place" in the journal *Language in Society*. Lakoff wrote: "the marginality and powerlessness of women is reflected in both the ways women are expected to speak, and the ways in which women are spoken of." Recognizing that "social mores as well as . . . purely linguistic data" were involved, she concluded that women's speech differed from men's. The article explored color distinction, expletives, and tag questions in particular. Lakoff concluded that women were more likely than men to distinguish cerise from mauve, to use "Oh my" or "Oh dear" instead of "Dammit," or to rephrase a statement into a question ("the situation is a problem, *isn't it?*"). Lakoff's work was based largely on her own observations rather than on an organized study, but it generated significant interest and reaction in the academy and in the popular consciousness. Linguists began the systematic study of the words and speech habits of women and men. And a ripple of change in common usage accompanied these efforts; firemen became firefighters, postmen became letter carriers, and department chairmen became just chairs. In the 1980s Georgetown scholar Deborah Tannen consolidated the work Lakoff and others had created over the previous decade and delivered to the popular consciousness a clear thesis about differences in the language of men and women: men talk to deliver information and women talk to create relationships. Tannen called these two styles rapport talk and report talk. She suggested that many of the speech habits of men and women were the result of this difference.

Both Lakoff and Tannen, with other scholarly researchers in this field, presented their claims within a cautionary framework. Nevertheless, the popular wisdom drawn from their work has consistently been taken to be a rigid rule about gender and speech. Men say this. Women say that. Men say "Goddammit." Women say "Oh my." Men don't ask for directions. Women ask questions. Men talk to deliver information. Women talk to make friends. The title of John Gray's book says it clearly: *Men Are from Mars, Women Are from Venus.* Men and women live in two entirely different worlds.

Early researchers in the field of gender and language were motivated, at least in part, by commitment to equal rights and equal access for women and men. Their studies were concurrent with a nationwide reexamination of discriminatory laws,

wages, and hiring practices. And yet, popular commentators focused primarily on the comic fringes of revision (Cooper-person for Cooperman, herstory for history) and magazines published bullet-pointed lists that divided the world of words: women smile and nod, men present a straight face; women relate through shared experiences, men relate through banter and silence; women use personal anecdotes, men use sports metaphors; women are tentative and apologetic, men are bold; women talk too much, men are concise. Such simplifications produced a lot of "shorthand" thinking, the kind of generalization that underlies prejudice. "It's a guy thing" was an easy way to dismiss someone else's concern without considering its legitimacy. And you've probably noticed that when someone wants to mock another person's idea, they usually raise the pitch of their voice to do this. Does sounding more like a woman make a speaker sound more ridiculous?

The polarized world of Mars and Venus had other troubling aspects. With the division of speech patterns into men's talk and women's talk came the implication that one way was better than the other. Women's ways were tentative, their expletives weak ("Good gracious"), and their statements hesitant ("These numbers aren't right, are they?"). Women were stereotyped as masters of moderation, euphemism, and uncertainty. Men were cast as the power brokers, comfortable with statements, advice, and silence. The solution seemed to be for women to adopt the speech habits of men. The male model must be the right way to say things. Margaret Thatcher was persuaded by her media consultant, Gordon Reece, to lower the pitch of her voice to increase her political credibility. *The Ladies Home Journal* and similar magazines of the day told women to adopt masculine speech habits as a shortcut to promotion. And teen magazines told girls they needed to play team sports, not for their health and pleasure, but so they could take risks, work in teams, win, lose, and use metaphors like "full court press" in the boardroom. (Fortunately, no one went so far as to instruct women to drive in endless circles around their target destination to show they didn't need to ask for directions.)

In the popular press, tough-guy negotiation skills and sports metaphors were repeatedly offered as important training—for women. As with books like *Women Who Love Too Much*—which might have been titled *Men Who Abuse Their Partners*—the solving of problems seemed to be women's work. Even now, this corrective initiative survives. Tina Flaherty's 1999 handbook *Talk Your Way to the Top* suggests every woman should "think like a woman and talk like a man." Books and articles of advice still target women and what women need to learn.

Do men and women speak alike? Sometimes. Is their speech distinguishable? Sometimes. Solid evidence exists mostly for differences like pitch and range of sound: women's voices are generally higher and employ a broader range of pitches (hence the recommendation made to Margaret Thatcher to lower her voice's pitch as a way to fit in a man's world of politics). There seems to be a fair body of evidence that women are more likely to choose the "prestige variant"—that is, to follow the rules more closely—in a given speech situation like the who/whom distinction or the full "ing" sound at the end of words like "walking," "talking," and "fixing." But gender doesn't influence speech in any invariable or easily documented way.

Lakoff, Tannen, and the pop psychologists who borrowed from them were talking about real differences in speech habits, but they read the text backward. Language differences aren't the result of gender. Language differences are learned. It is cultural differences—differences in the lives and experiences of individuals—that make the differences in how we talk. If a friend recommends a doctor, and you ask, "What's his name," your assumption is not a random one. Because most doctors are men, using "he" or "his" as the generic has a basis in the real situation of the medical profession. But as the composition of a workforce changes—for example, among airline flight attendants—the language makes the accommodation. Hence, the demise of the term "stewardess." Language is more a mirror than a mold.

As long as our culture constructs each gender differently, expecting different things from boys and girls, allowing different behaviors in men and women—if boldness and aggression are associated with boys and politeness and tentativeness are associated with girls—the speech of women and men will reflect such differences. Where other behaviors are encouraged or sought, other speech will prevail. Culture is a more powerful and more comprehensive force than gender; pressures from geography, age, position, and expectation are part of the formula. Men and women? How about media consultant and social worker? There's Mars and Venus for you! Or talk to a veteran male priest from rural South Carolina and a young female investment banker from New York City. Gender may have some impact on their speech choices, but other influences are at work. Don't expect her to ask after your kids.

Remember Emlyn Anderson? Anderson began her job at Ahern Architectural Associates with great expectations and a sense that she would have limitless opportunities to put her computer design skills to work. But her boss, Jack Lanzo, wasn't able to give her much freedom to prove herself. Every time someone asked a question or conferred with Anderson, Lanzo was all over the conversation. Anderson might easily conclude that Lanzo didn't think that she was competent enough to handle the work herself and thus decide he was a sexist who discounted her abilities because she was a woman.

But what about her age? At twenty-four, she seems like a youngster to Lanzo (in fact, rather like Lanzo's own college-age daughter). Lanzo's been in the business for more than thirty years so he feels he should jump into conversations where he can anticipate the problems. Since his department competes with other internal groups, he needs to look good. He wants to help her avoid making mistakes (she'll probably make some). Anderson's degree from Yale is part of this "situation," too. She talks about software programs Lanzo has never used. She wrote her master's thesis on design options for a multiuse theater and performing arts complex in Bangkok. Lanzo moved up the ladder by effort rather than education, starting as a draftsman. He finds some of the things Anderson talks about confusing and, to him, irrelevant. Every conversation between Lanzo and Anderson is affected by her knowledge that he is her boss, her senior, and a self-made man. His comments take into account her age, her gender, and her education.

Or consider the claim of Naomi Wolf, a writer and a consultant to Al Gore's campaign committee. In a 1993 *New Republic* article, Wolf suggested that strong opinions were more the province of men. She found that men express their opinions in public forums more often than do women. She cited 55 female guests on *Crossfire* in 1992 as compared with 440 male guests. She found during a one-month period in 1992 that 84 percent of op-ed pieces in *The New York Times* were by men. Her editors received eight unsolicited articles by women in October of 1993 compared with fifty-five submitted by men. But Wolf, in this article, did her homework, made a claim, marshaled support for her point of view, and even chastised her publisher for underrepresenting women. She wasn't afraid of an argument, although her research suggested she should be. Even if there are more male than female doctors, more female than male therapists, a history of gender difference, or a long tradition of style and habit to deal with, the language strategies of *Power Talk* are available to everyone.

The English language itself cannot be declared the "enemy." Language won't take the rap for the differences Lakoff, Tannen, and other sociolinguists described because social injustice isn't a matter of grammar and word choice. Notice the evolution of a racial designation in the United States: colored to Negro to black to African American. The names have changed, but this sequence of changes has not eliminated prejudice and racism. The search-and-replace mentality changes words, not hearts. If we study the speech styles of women and men, we need a clear understanding of what is cause and what is effect, what is determined by biology, what is learned from culture, and what is open to choice.

We all have a core speech style, a default setting learned in our homes, our hometowns, our homelands. We speak, drawing on a fairly predictable and regularized repertoire of constructions, words, and phrases. But we adjust our speech in every conversation we enter. Lining the world up into the girls and the guys overlooks how complicated and how variable our choices are. It reinforces the enormous prejudice that language differences sometimes generate. It perpetuates stereotypes. And it denies us options to grow, change, or experiment.

The preeminent sociolinguist William Labov didn't like the term "sociolinguistics." He felt it implied there was a language study that could be somehow separated from the social context. To him, all meaningful language study considers an array of social factors surrounding a statement. One of these is gender. Another is geography. Then there's age, race, education, class, position, assumptions, values, and topic. Who's in charge when adults speak to children? How about when Grandad needs Billy's help with the computer? Who's got the power when non-native speakers of a language try to be heard? How about when you're sitting at their conference table?

No one feature creates misunderstandings or influences speakers to choose the words they use. An analysis of power, however, captures a majority of the features and their interaction. Identifying Language from the Center and Language from the Edge provides an easy way to think about the politics of a given conversation. And replacing the gender idea with a power analysis not only eliminates a destructive, divisive force in the conversation, it sidesteps the sense of inevitability and determinism that the gender argument creates. Finally, it engages each of us in the process of "language in a social context." By talking and thinking about Language from the Center and Language from the Edge, each speaker and listener can assess how the leader has taken control, how he or she is maintaining power, and what might be the best means to access the power. Thus we can continue to study the politics of language and the sociology of power without excluding anyone from access to power or to powerful speech strategies.

WHERE GENDER MAKES A DIFFERENCE

If the speech variations for men and women are minimal, if their language options are the same, does that mean their lives and experiences are the same? No. And as we have seen, language differences grow from cultural differences. In her comprehensive and enlightening book *Why So Slow?* psychologist and educator Virginia Valian reviews the research of the last two decades and summarizes the conclusions of a multitude of studies in the education, working conditions, and life experiences of women and men. It is the lives of men and women, rather than their speech, that can seem galaxies apart. The significant differences are not linguistic, but economic, cultural, and psychological. Valian cites studies (usually several in support of each) to demonstrate that:

1. Women internalize failure more than men.
2. Women are less influential than men in a group decision.
3. Attractiveness has a negative impact on the perception of a woman's competence and a positive impact on the perception of a man's competence.
4. Both men and women elicit negative response when they are assertive or try to solve a problem but women are judged more negatively than men.
5. Women's successes are more likely to be attributed to luck than to skill; men's successes are more likely to be attributed to skill than to luck.
6. Women expect to receive fewer benefits from their work than men do.
7. Women often overestimate the difficulty of a task; men often underestimate the difficulty of a task.
8. Women, when they talk, are attended to less than men by both men and women.

Discussions of language and gender have been influenced, of course, by findings such as these and the differences they corroborate. But only the finding that women are not as likely to be listened to can be said to relate directly to language research. And even this is complicated by other factors like age. A female TV executive in her early thirties commented on her work situation: "I have no difficulty communicating with males under thirty-five. But those guys [men over thirty-five] I rarely can easily communicate with. They don't hear me." Then there's rank. Janet Reno and Madeleine Albright are listened to. And don't forget, this "being heard" issue has been around for a while. Even the young Queen Elizabeth I struggled to have her say (this was in 1558). At the age of twenty-five she inherited control of a bankrupt and divided nation. Many thought she needed advice; most thought she needed a husband. Historian David Willson explains how she managed her advisers and her Council:

> She feared that in the give-and-take of discussion she might be overruled; her practice was to have problems debated in the Council and its advice brought to her, so that she could accept or reject that advice as she saw fit. Much of her governing was done in private interviews with one or two of her ministers.

Despite the Renaissance turf wars, her gender, and her age, she built power. Ultimately, the Spanish ambassador wrote that she was "incomparably more feared than her sister, and gives her orders and has her way as absolutely as her father did."

Men may need to focus their attention more when women speak. Women may need to consider alternative ways to be heard if the standard procedures of a meeting leave them unnoticed. These suggestions apply to any conversational dynamic: man or woman, if you aren't getting heard, if you're relegated to the edge rather than being there by choice, do something about it. If you take heat for taking the floor, get over it. Linda Greenlaw, a swordfish-boat captain and author of *The Hungry Ocean*, offers good advice based on her success in a business where sex-discrimination might seem inevitable: "I'm not easily offended."

As Valian points out, the negative reactions aren't just for women. Aggressive speech elicits criticism no matter who uses it. The reaction is just more intense against women. Donna Demizio may be experiencing some fallout because she talks a lot—and she's a woman. Susan McCann may have been lectured about her rudeness in part because she chose to present herself as a competent woman on the inside track with the boss. Women who choose Language from the Center can be criticized for it, particularly by other women. But the price of nice is silence. If McCann decides to take Louise's advice to heart, she will never be at the center and she will never be heard.

Even if the "make no waves" style appeals to you, remember it's not conflict-free. Involving everyone in every decision is time-consuming. Neil Rudenstein, president of Harvard, took a health leave in 1994 to recover from the exhaustion of listening to every voice in his huge institution. And for women in leadership positions, Language from the Edge can seem like the worst parts of feminine stereotyping. An agent who worked closely with former ABC-TV president Jamie Tarses commented on her style: "This may sound sexist, but women are emotional and Jamie is particularly emotional. You think of her as a girl, and it changes how you do business with her. We'll have a meeting and I can tell if she's hurt by something, like I've wounded her personally. It's just business with [the men]. With Jamie, it's more like dating." Whether the emotional style is a woman's style or just Tarses's style, it is assigned to her gender and used to criticize her.

Rita Simon, University Professor of Justice, Law, and Society at American University, examined extensive public policy data and found that the major disagreements recorded there related not to gender, but to race, ethnicity, and class. Simon wrote: "National public-opinion data on a whole range of policy questions show no significant differences in the beliefs and attitudes of men and women. The major disagreements revealed by the data stem from racial, ethnic, and class differences, not sex." Simon pointed to college campuses as immediate evidence of these kinds of disagreements.

In sum, gender does not account for all that is going on in communication and miscommunication in relationships or in the workplace. Sometimes men and women don't make sense to each other. Sometimes they don't make sense to anyone. If the bombing of the Chinese embassy in Belgrade was easily explainable, the trade talks wouldn't have stalled for half a year. The pilots may have felt their seniority demanded knowledge of the targets. Or their role as specially selected pilots in a military action, rather than their gender, may have kept them from asking for multiple cross-checks of the map. Or things may have just happened very fast. But "the guy thing" was the easy answer. If gender figures into the problem, it's only one part of the answer. The full spectrum of situational factors is the rest. William Labov summarized nicely what we know and what we need to remember about the differences of speech as determined by gender: "The real differences that have been studied are very minor, but perhaps symbolically they have become very important."

Chapter Eight
A World of
Difference

"No individual, no country, no people, no history of a people, no state is like any other. Therefore, the true, the beautiful and the good are not the same for them."

J. G. Herder

Even when we think we're on the home planet, we may not be in familiar territory. Consider the senior project manager from a New York consulting firm who heads to Winston-Salem, North Carolina, to meet with clients at First Wachovia Bank. He has an important presentation to make and fog at La Guardia makes the timing tight. But the meeting isn't going to start without him. The cab does its part. He arrives at his destination with three minutes to spare. He is met by his North Carolina counterpart and the two head for the private elevator to the executive dining room. They press the button. Nothing lights up. Nothing goes "ping." Inscribed under the buttons they see: ACCESS KEY REQUIRED.

"Dammit . . . get somebody on this," says the New Yorker. But the North Carolina contact has never been to the executive dining room before and has no idea how (or who) to get on it. They are now officially late and the senior manager is running out of patience. He wants control here and Language from the Center makes him feel like he's got it.

Both men look around in desperation. Ambling toward them, they see a bank guard, an enormous Pillsbury Doughboy in blue. From his belt sparkles a silver smile of keys. The consultant prepares to pounce. But the local counterpart steps in front of him and motions silence. They stand quietly and wait as the guard approaches.

"Hey," smiles the local, as though this were a chance encounter on a country road.

"And what might I do for you two fine gentlemen today?" offers the guard.

"Well, we're in a bit of a mess here. I mashed this button but nothin's happenin'," begins the local. Then he smiles at the guard. In a few seconds, everyone is on the way to the dining room. The New Yorker isn't in Bombay; he isn't even in a different time zone. Still, the guidance of his North Carolina contact is indispensable. Without it, he would have relied on his default position: "Dammit, I need to be upstairs right now—get me into this elevator." And a "who's in charge here" standoff might have added to the delay. Headed south, the consultant knew his speech would sound different. But he didn't think much about the local language, the differences in conversational conventions. The familiarity of the greeting, the recognizable local idiom, the informality of "happenin'" saved the day here and produced the keys.

Gender has little to do with this scenario. But a multitude of other situational factors—geography, rank, assumption, class, education—are at work. So while Language from the Center and Language from the Edge help sort out the politics of a situation, the time, place, and persons involved also need to be considered. Gender has received the majority of popular media attention, but cultural conventions often are more significant factors in confusions, misunderstandings, and mistakes. And while everyone remembers to pack a phrase book for multilingual meetings, it's easy to forget these cultural differences where speakers all use English. The challenge of listening carefully and of being understood can be even more elusive when the assumption is "we all speak the same language."

The Politics of Language

As with the consultant from New York, geography makes a difference. These regional differences in English are familiar (remember Adam and Lagwadia). They have had a long history of scrutiny. In the dim past, different languages were, after all, dialects of a single language (for example, French and Spanish began as geographic dialects of Latin). Subtle sound variations survive: do you say "greasy" or "greazy"? "Mirror" or "mere"? "Ex-pair-a-mint" or "ex-spear-a-mint"? Pace, volume, the habit of interruption—the pace of speech in California versus New York City, the length of pauses in the Northeast and the Southwest, protocols of conversation in rural areas and in cities—vary among speakers of the same language. John Adams, living in Boston, wrote of New Yorkers: "They talk loud, very fast, and all together. If they ask you a question, before you can utter three words of your answer, they will break out upon you again . . . and talk away." That was in 1774.

We treasure the sound and style of our own conversation. We like to notice everyone else's "accent." And as with the popular view of gender differences—where men's ways have been touted to women—geography has its pecking order. For several decades, TV broadcasters were told that a Midwestern dialect was "pure," unaccented, and the ideal media speech. But, in fact, there are specific vowel sounds that distinguish the American midlands. And Chicagoans' pronunciation of their football team—"*da*-bares"—is just one bit of evidence that the Midwest has its own way of saying things. True, certain pronunciations are valued over others: thee-*ay*-ter, *poh*-lice, wa*r*sh, and pa*h*k (for wash and park) are regularly seen as inferior. Urban accents are distrusted more than rural ones. "Correct" English—the prestige variant—works well in the classroom, but the average fifteen-year-old boy is wise enough to give it up on the playground. And we all know at least one British-American who, after ten years in the United States, still retains a London accent. There's a hierarchy within every subset. Saturday morning cartoon characters like Warner Brothers' Foghorn

Leghorn, Mindy on *Animaniacs*, or the superhero villains offer their own set of accents associated with stupidity, evil, and innocence. For me, growing up in New Jersey meant endless defenses of Hoboken, the state's transportation system, and the fact that no one in New Jersey says New "Joisey." I'd explain that New "Joisey" is what urban New Yorkers in the boroughs say—loss of "r" isn't typical of Middle Atlantic speech. Regional speech characteristics, however, are often labeled "nasal" or "guttural," terms with little meaning in formal language study but ones that often reflect narrow judgments about class, race, and education. We all say "I don't have an accent" until we listen with educated ears.

Thus language differences both unify and divide us. The Bible gives us the story of the Gileadites. This tribe determined who belonged and who didn't by the pronunciation of the Hebrew word "shibboleth." And we still call on speech differences to sort out those who belong. Think of the child transplanted to a new state (or even to a new school) who feels the sting of "You talk funny." Or Scots pressured to speak London English, South Boston kids sent looking for their lost "r"s, or provincial French speakers urged to copy the dialect of Paris. In the 1950s, it was not unusual for commentators to judge Black Vernacular English as deficient. Some educators believed that speakers of Black English lacked a true understanding of language. They recommended instruction in the formation of verbs and plurals. Black English, however, is as rule-bound and consistent as any language. James Baldwin's essay "If Black English Isn't a Language, Then Tell Me, What Is?" is one of several articulate defenses of this language variety. Black English is not spoken by all African Americans in this country and has its own geographic distribution. But in our world of rap music, rock stars, and hip-hop, everyone now borrows "He got game," "You go, girl," and "Yo momma."

The hierarchy of prestige and the implied judgment of "correctness" marks one group for inclusion and demands another to conform. Armed with the sense that what I do must be right (it's written down somewhere, I'm sure), I can claim an extra share of whatever power is going around. Efforts to expand beyond or change the prescribed forms and agreed-upon (whatever that means) standards run the risk of looking like mistakes rather than open-minded flexibility. We all say "He flied out to center field" but those who can explain why it's correct occupy a special place in grammar heaven. Important social policies depend on these judgments, however. Ongoing battles about bilingual education, about recognizing Black English in classrooms, about making English the official language of the country reveal hierarchies and the distribution of power in contemporary culture. "Correctness" is the enforcer. Perhaps this is why teenagers can fool around with language more than anyone else—they live to break rules.

A WELTER OF ENGLISHES

A knowledge of subtle situational factors can help all speakers get beyond their own little world, an important skill in the global village of today's commerce. This is where the speakers of English, drawing on different cultural conventions, can feel like they're on a planet more distant even than Venus. Sociolinguist John Gumperz studied such a case at a London-area airport. In the commissary, the Indian and Pakistani women who served food to baggage handlers were unhappy in their work. They complained of rudeness from the men they served. But the baggage handlers themselves weren't satisfied with the food service. They found the servers unhelpful and unfriendly. Men and women at odds? New populations versus old? In an analysis of cross-cultural communication among these workers, Gumperz found that the problem was created by a small difference in speech style. The food workers did not use a rising inflection when they offered things to the hungry baggage handlers. If a meal included gravy, the women said, "Gravy." As English was not their native language, they did not use the subtle convention of asking a question with a rising inflection. The baggage handlers expected to be offered—"Gravy?" They felt they were being treated rudely. The women wondered why they received such negative responses. Everyone was speaking English. This small variation in inflection made communication difficult. Where one or more speakers are using a second language, such differences are easy to overlook—and sometimes they are significant.

All companies are, in some sense, international. So speakers of English as a second language are now a part of everyone's life and work. Even the most local industries must consider Japanese technology, European investors, and the fiscal health of Brazil; utility companies, banks, and law offices seek an international presence. The dominance of English in the business world has made those who speak it as a first language complacent and less motivated to master other languages. Like former member of British Parliament and literature scholar Enoch Powell, they might say, "Others may speak and read English—more or less—but it is our language and not theirs." Such a claim makes little sense today: our need to share English and to understand other languages is critical. The European Union already accommodates the eleven languages of its fifteen countries; they will need to add five more translators if eastern and central European nations join the group.

Just understanding other speakers of English is tough enough. In *Fatal Words: Communication Clashes and Aircraft Crashes,* Steven Cushing recounts incidents like the 1977 Tenerife collision that resulted in six hundred deaths. The pilot radioed: "We are now at takeoff." The tower took this to mean the plane was waiting on the runway, but in fact the plane was at liftoff. The frequency of such misunderstandings is cause for concern (and sufficient to fill a 162-page book); it has led researchers at Cambridge University in England to begin developing "operational languages" designed to make critical international conversations less subject to error.

THE BRITISH ARE COMING

But even when we restrict the conversation to speakers of English, exactly what English are we using?

From the *New York Review of Books*:

> Petite, pretty blond professional seeks relationship built around laughter, love and a view that life should continue to be an adventure.

From the *London Review of Books*:

> Insensitive 47-year-old lounge lizard (male), seeks woman with energy to suffer periods of self-indulgence. Offers in return good sangria and complete lack of interest in sport.

Speakers of English—from Britain, Ireland, America, Canada, Australia, New Zealand, or parts of South Africa—share words and meanings, but again, not all the conventions of language. Phil Driscoll, former director of sales and marketing for TWA's international operation, worked with British colleagues in what he came to view as a bilingual job involving British English and American English. "I looked at these two 'languages' as about as different as Spanish and Portuguese," says Driscoll. And the pecking order applies, too. "I knew to defer to the British forms. I was stationed in Heathrow, after all," Driscoll recalls.

A university student's efforts to find a job further demonstrates these unacknowledged elements of communication. In the hiring rounds at his college, Michael O'Neill signed up for interviews with the New York investment banks that yearly hire twenty to twenty-five seniors. O'Neill had no trouble getting interviews. His grades in economics were solid and his summers had been spent as an intern in a bank in his native Dublin. At the end of the second round, however, O'Neill had no job offers. One of the interviewers explained: "Yes, he's got the credentials, but we're looking for an aggressive personality, someone who'll run through brick walls. He just didn't seem to want this enough." But O'Neill's problem wasn't motivation. Cultural conventions of speech and behavior played the lead role in this story. O'Neill's conversational style, despite four years at an American college, was founded on Language from the Edge and a deference he had learned at home and in his parochial high school. Swaggering, challenging, contradicting, or taking over the conversation did not occur to him. But his interviewers were looking for Language from the Center from the job applicant. Over the holiday break, however, O'Neill took a sequence of interviews in London; three banks made offers. "We don't want some arrogant twerp stepping on toes here," said the British recruiter. "The New York style may work well there but it doesn't work well here. We want a deferential type, a listener, someone who can build relationships . . . not a video game cowboy who only wants to score enough points to get to the next level."

Conversely, after Dwight Allen spent eleven years analyzing companies in New York City, he landed in the bank's London office. Allen found "they don't count by deals in Europe." This meant a different way of talking business. "I realized the long-term relationship counted more," he says. Allen learned to personalize everything and put the relationship ahead of the information blitz. Knowing that constant content-free updates were less important than a sense of real attention, Allen slowed down and tailored his style to his audience. Language from the Center was what he was used to; he adopted Language from the Edge. Both O'Neill and Allen thought they knew "the local language." Both of them, however, had adjustments to make.

English as a Foreign Language

Today more people speak English as a foreign language than speak it as a native language. Some know English from classroom instruction. Others know English from American television and movies like *Die Hard*. Lindsley Medlin, vice president and managing director of the European operations of Priority Fulfillment Services Europe, found he had to set a few coworkers straight about using profanities that seemed like normal conversation to those who had watched countless American movie videos. And he had to correct one well-meaning colleague who thought he knew a witty American epigram: "We have a policy here: keep it stupid, simple."

Of course, many speakers learn English only on the job—in uses relevant to their work—knowing "crayons" only as supercomputers or "gilts" only as pigs. Barry Newman, in a 1993 *Wall Street Journal* article, investigated the purpose-built English used in places like the Prague office of the Japanese auto company Daihatsu. All conversations with the managing director take place in English. But neither the director nor his Czech staff use or understand idiomatic expressions like "touch base," "run it up the flagpole," "max out," or "blow this deal." Newman's article describes an interviewer who repeatedly said "Really" as an applicant described his experiences and talents. The applicant thought he was being accused of lying. Another candidate was entirely confused when he said he had some questions and his American interviewer responded, "Fire away."

Where both speakers are using English as a second language, even more care is required. Alan Firth, at the University of Aalborg in Denmark, studies the confusions that occur in such situations. He recorded a conversation between a German and an Egyptian, about an order of cheese. Both men used English, although neither spoke it as a first language:

> "So I told him not to send the cheese after the blowing in customs."
>
> "I see, yes." [although the exporter is wondering what "blowing" means here]
>
> "So I don't know what we can do with the order now."

"I'm not, er, blowing, er, what, er, what is this, er, too big or what?"

"No, the cheese is bad. It is, like, fermenting in the customs' cool rooms."

"Ah, it's gone off!"

"Yes, it's gone off."

Gone off, blowing, bad. All different expressions with the same meaning, but meanings not shared between the Egyptian and German speakers.

Subtle conventions about crossing legs, putting your arm around someone, even the style of presenting information vary from culture to culture. In one place, argument may be part of every conversation, even if there is agreement all around. In another, argument may be fatal to the deal. Craig Weeks, a vice president posted to Geneva for a trading company, discovered, "You have to approach things from the side. Attack strategies don't play well. In fact, even a sense of that strategy can ruin a conversation." Words can go one way while the nodding head or the smiling face mean something else. Humor, nuance, and sarcasm are learned more slowly than the core vocabulary of a language.

Thinking about Language from the Center and from the Edge may help in the adjustment to different cultural conventions. But remembering all aspects of speech—the words and delivery, the letter and the envelope—will help. "You need to be able to accept difference," suggests Medlin. The adjustments can be large and small. A demeaning term for gays or job listings that ask for "a good-looking young woman" may offend you. Sensitivity to cultural differences doesn't require imitation, but it may require thick skin. Choose the battles wisely. You are there to get a signed contract, not to change the world. As Weeks's wife and coadventurer, Lorrie, says, "Some days, quaint turns out to be just inconvenient."

IN A WORLD OF DIFFERENCE, MAKE A DIFFERENCE

Communications professor Donald Rubin had two groups of college students listen to a brief lecture by a native speaker of English. During the lesson, each group was shown a projected photograph of a person they were told was the speaker. The students who thought they were listening to a native speaker of English understood the material better than those who assumed their lecture was being delivered by a non-native speaker. Yet both groups listened to the same tape.

We all need to work together. Rigid visions of correctness block such cooperation. Like English teachers gone bad, we are tempted to dismiss what sounds "wrong" or unfamiliar. But our understanding of language difference is most useful and most flexible when factors of gender, age, place, race, education, class, and authority are all considered. Knowing all the factors that shape language choice allows you to consciously set aside judgment of people whose speech style is different. Where the differences are unrelated to content or meaning, small pronunciation differences are irrelevant. Tolerance of different accents, word choices, and speech conventions is a way to embrace diversity and combat prejudice.

If we consider Language from the Center and Language from the Edge, rather than the language of men versus women, black versus white, native speaker versus non-native speaker, we can parse out the real power distribution in the situation. We can't eliminate the fact that some groups have historically held greater power than others. But we can eliminate a destructive, divisive force in the conversation as well as a sense of inevitability and powerlessness about speech choices.

From the beginning, my claim has been that language is situational. It is not just one but a multitude of factors that determines what we say. From an array of options, we concoct the selves we present in each situation. The words we choose are part of what social psychologist Erving Goffman calls "impression management." The constellation of influences designated here as "power" is not the one thing needed to explain the complicated phenomenon of human expression. The concept of Language from the Center and Language from the Edge doesn't cover the whole territory of language. But it's a useful way to look at the politics of language. And it's a concept we can all employ to enrich our understanding of the world of work.

Ultimately, education should improve the world of the learner. In a world of difference, we can make a difference. If we are observant of language features that relate to our own geography, education, race, culture, and age, we can be more tolerant of difference. If we resist the temptation to use "correctness" as an easy means to exclude, we can uncover the best ideas. If we remember that changing words won't change minds, that speakers who only adjust their language—who substitute "The women in the front office" for "The girls in the front office" or who adopt "international visitors" for "foreigners"—don't necessarily adjust their thinking, we can name our problems accurately. Language study can make us heard—and can open our ears as we listen to each other.

HEADS-UP

1. Be observant of language habits that relate to your own geography, age, and education.
2. Be tolerant of difference.
3. Don't make quick judgments based on accents, varieties, or assumptions about "correctness."
4. In speaking to novice users of English, provide several words for what isn't understood. Be flexible. Synonyms work better than repetitions and increased volume.
5. Where you are a visitor, your situation puts you on the edge. Ask questions and defer to other speakers until you know the extent of your power. Sellers adapt to buyers but it helps when everyone is working on adaptation. And remember that Language from the Edge doesn't be-

long to one gender. Anyone can work with this responsive and collaborative style.

6. Don't assume high school language study will equip you for complicated or delicate negotiations. Spanish isn't Portuguese, Mexico City isn't Madrid, Quebec isn't Paris: do your homework.

7. In initial conversations, avoid slang, acronyms, and colloquial expressions. Both speakers need to understand a language well to share humor, sarcasm, and subtlety. You can test the waters with simple vocabulary.

8. Don't be afraid of pauses in conversations. Don't hesitate to ask for clarifications, but clarify politely. Expect mistakes on both sides.

9. Remember, in multilingual settings, written agreements are more reliable than spoken ones.

10. Hire an interpreter for important conversations where your (or their) mastery of the other language is incomplete. Choose one whose first language is theirs.

11. Anticipate trouble. "Visiting firemen" from central office may be significantly behind in understanding the conventions you've mastered in the international location. Prepare them to look good.

12. Remember those you've brought along. Your partner, wife, husband, or children will struggle to adjust (without recourse to an assistant in the outer office). Young children will be masters of the new language first.

13. Be sensitive to cultural difference; choose your battles carefully. Don't mimic blindly. Don't try to change the world in one trip, either.

14. Learn other languages. At the very least, master the basic phrases of greeting and thanks. John F. Kennedy's *"Ich bin ein Berliner"* may have meant "I'm a pastry" but that small effort pleased his audience and demonstrated his effort to connect to them.

Chapter Nine
The Study of Linguistics

On February 4, 1997, Louise Woodward, a British nanny working for an American family in Newton, Massachusetts, dialed 911. Police arrived and found a severely injured child. In questioning Woodward, police recorded her statement: "I dropped him onto the floor." Five days later, Matthew Eappen died at Children's Hospital, Boston, and Woodward was indicted for his murder. During the trial, Woodward stated that she had, in fact, said, "I popped him onto the floor." In the language of her north England village, the expression means "I put him on the floor." The police heard "dropped." The prosecutor asked, "Is it just a coincidence that 'popped' sounds a lot like 'dropped'?" To him, "popped" might as easily have meant dropped, threw, or even slammed. In Woodward's case, sound and sense—points of phonology, semantics, and regional dialect—were matters of life and death.

In this book, linguistics has been considered primarily in its social context. The motive for this consideration has been the analysis of power and influence. Previous chapters have looked at the daily conversations of work, the role of situation in those conversations, and some strategies for successful negotiation. How speech choices affect our work, our relationships, and our understanding of the world around us can, as in the Woodward case, take on determining significance. A fuller understanding of linguistics as a field of study—of semantics, phonology, syntax, word history—offers a healthy respect for the complexities of language, a solid admiration for the powers of the human mind, and an appropriate tolerance for differences.

Afraid someone's going to tell you that you just split an infinitive? Not surprising. This is the commonest reaction to conversations about language. But knowing about when people began to study language and how this study has developed accounts for that impulse as well as its limits. This chapter offers a more complete picture for those who want to know what the discipline of linguistics is all about and for those who collect interesting stories about dictionaries, Sanskrit, alphabets, and wugs.

History

The beginning of English language study was founded on notions about fixing, correcting, and cleaning up the language. These efforts, in the early 1600s, inspired several simple dictionaries designed to teach "the true writing" and, over the next several centuries, many books of grammatical instruction. Many agreed with Jonathan Swift who, in 1712, found "our language . . . extremely imperfect" and in need of correction. Of course, there were those who understood the difficulty of such efforts to control and contain. In the preface to his great dictionary of 1755, Samuel Johnson acknowledged: "[N]o dictionary of a living tongue ever can be perfect, since while it is hastening to publication, some words are budding and some falling away." Even today, most school instruction follows the lead of prescriptive linguistics and takes courage from the annual crop of articles about how the world is going to hell in a handbasket with language leading the way.

Fortunately, in the nineteenth century, literacy and international trade broadened the focus of language study from these collecting and corrective purposes. English scholars began to classify and compare languages. Scholars like Jacob Grimm and Rasmus Rask formulated rules and theories based on the discovery of similarities among ancient and modern languages (collecting Grimms' fairy tales along the way). Researchers speculated about common sources for languages as seemingly unrelated as Lithuanian and Sanskrit or Yiddish and Afrikaans. By comparing languages and tracing the historical development of English, scholars were able to postulate a sort of genealogy of human language. They reconstructed the sources (protolanguages) of modern languages and asked questions about historical rather than prescriptive linguistics.

DESCRIPTIVE LINGUISTICS

By the mid-twentieth century, however, linguists were exploring entirely new territory, building a geography of American English regional dialects, researching the meaning of "lame" in Black Vernacular English, listening to adolescents and their slang, and considering the conventions and assumptions involved in "How are you?" Linguistics as we know it today is as much concerned with new areas of research as with the centuries-old business of constructing language families.

SYSTEMS

"Colorless green ideas sleep furiously." In the 1950s, MIT professor Noam Chomsky used this sentence to change how we think about sentences. What does it mean? Hard to say—and yet, even though the words as combined do not yield a clear idea, the organization—the grammatical sense of the sentence—is real. We are tempted to ask, "What do you mean by 'sleep'?" or "Is this part of a poem?" We cannot decode the meaning, but we recognize an English sentence. Chomsky used "Colorless green ideas sleep furiously" to demonstrate the presence of the mental rules that allow us to distinguish grammatical (if nonsensical) sentences from nongrammatical nonsense (like "Dog pleasant the toward after breeze"). His transformational grammar revolutionized traditional thinking about the mental operations of grammar and the relationships among languages.

SOCIOLINGUISTICS

In the last fifty years, the study of language has grown and diversified. While earlier researchers sought the details of language history or the universals of mental grammar, scholars like William Labov, at the University of Pennsylvania, looked at language in use. With other sociolinguists, he examined how class, gender, age, and ethnicity influence what we say and how we understand each other. For example, Labov looked for a correlation between the prestige of three New York City department stores and the loss of "r" in the speech of their salespeople. By asking clerks for directions to something he knew was on the fourth floor, he found that the fancier stores had fewer clerks who said "foth flaw." Surprisingly, however, some clerks in the most exclusive departments of the most exclusive store, Saks Fifth Avenue, did demonstrate this classic New York City speech feature. From this, Labov fashioned the idea of linguistic security. If a longtime clerk in the fur department at Saks knows she's the top seller in the store, she isn't going to apologize for (or forsake) her background in Queens! Labov researched a multitude of other phenomena that fifty years before would not have been considered worthy of study. His sixties research, published as *The Social Stratification of English in New York City,* expanded the range of speech study to include questions of age, race, education, social status, aspiration, and prestige.

NEUROLOGY

Science has also revolutionized language study. Scanning equipment that allows researchers to study the brain has significantly enhanced our understanding of where language resides in the brain and what electromagnetic activities relate to speech and thought. While scientists formerly studied injury and trauma to guide their understanding of the connection between the brain and language production, MRIs and MRAs now allow researchers to observe the activity of healthy brains as subjects think and speak. Attention to language acquisition and second language learning for non-native speakers has improved our understanding of how children and adults process language as well. What we teach in our schools (curriculum) and how we present it to youngsters (pedagogy) incorporate these findings. While some researchers have charted the onset of speech, the sequence of learning, and the role of left-brain and right-brain, others are observing the decay of these skills over time—in stroke, aging, or Alzheimer's patients. Advances in computing have had an impact, too, providing models of specific linguistic theories. Programming languages borrow from and have also shed light on human languages. Researchers' interest in artificial intelligence suggests language may be the key to the creation of smart machines.

Okay, still there? Admittedly, this isn't as much fun as a video game. Nonetheless, it's interesting to discover that prescriptive linguistics—our motive to "improve" language—has a long history. It is where English language study began and it's not going away any time soon. Notice William Safire's conversion from political commentator to weekly language maven (one reflection on President Clinton's investigation by special prosecutor Kenneth Starr sorted out the proper pronunciation of the word "brooch"). The older generation still laments the language habits of youth and a few schoolteachers are still insisting on "May I" and "None of us is." But it's exciting to see how comparatively new is our interest in descriptive linguistics, language in everyday use.

Conversations about right and wrong lead most often to the discovery that things are changing. NationsBank is capitalizing a medial letter. Investment advisers warn, "The price is north of a million." The construction, "Each of us has their [not his] own copy" is making a stand for acceptance. And your new squash partner says, "You like totally almost had me!" Are these things right, wrong, or merely out there? Knowing the source and significance of these changes is part of a crash course in linguistics.

HISTORICAL LINGUISTICS

When and where did humans begin to speak? How complicated and how many were the earliest languages? How did these evolve and spread? Linguistics involves history. The study of such questions makes a curriculum full of branching tree diagrams and speculative protolanguages (see pages 170–171).

Studying words shared among a group of languages (for example, these instances of the number seven: French: *sept*, Italian: *sette*, Spanish: *siete*, Portuguese: *sétimo*, Slovak: *sedem*, Sanskrit: *sapta*) suggests a common source for the whole group. The absence of some words and the presence of others support speculation about a language's place of origin. A protolanguage with no word for palm tree, for example, but words for wolf and bear, birch and oak, might suggest a northern European location. Between all the hunting and the gathering, however, no one was writing anything down. How to assemble these language families and where to draw the lines is the work of historical linguists.

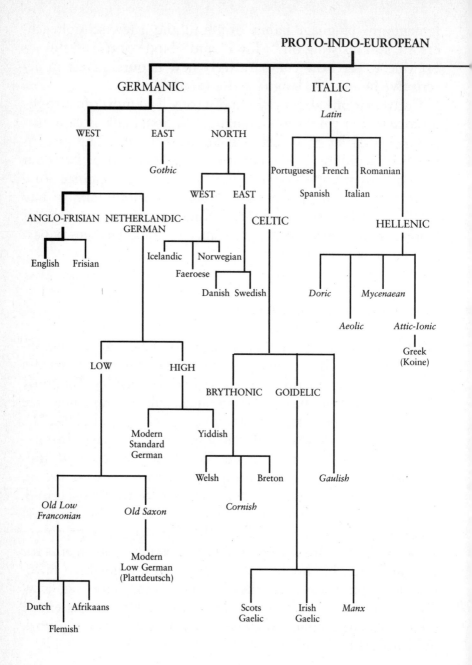

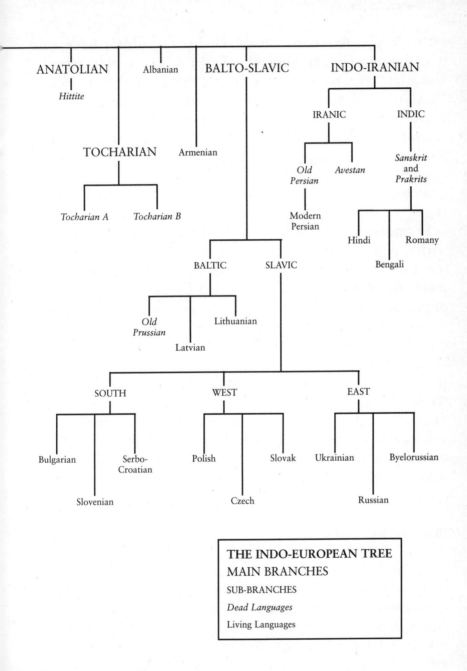

THE INDO-EUROPEAN TREE
MAIN BRANCHES
SUB-BRANCHES
Dead Languages
Living Languages

ETYMOLOGY

"It's okay to boycott jeeps." Dickens couldn't have said that. Etymology explains why. Did you know that "apron" was first "naperon," a word with connections to "napkin"? "Starve" meant to die and didn't specify the cause. "Flesh" could be the meat you'd serve for dinner. And "okay" (from a symbol of document approval), "boycott" (from an Irish land agent, Captain Charles Boycott), and "jeep" (from the military expression GP for "general purpose") are entirely new words introduced into English in the last hundred years.

Etymology, the study of word history, became possible with the invention of writing. The first English dictionary, in the early 1600s, began the work of recording words and their meanings. *The Oxford English Dictionary,* a dictionary organized according to historical principles—that is, designed to show changes in word meaning—was not produced until the end of the nineteenth century. In it, James A. H. Murray used a thousand years of English literature to trace the evolution of meanings like "handsome" (it used to mean "handy") and "let" (only in tennis does it still mean "to hold back"). Murray's work was the first complete and systematic gathering of word histories. The project, conceived as a ten-year job, took fifty years. Murray died working on the letter T.

ORTHOGRAPHY

Study of the code we use to transcribe our speech is called orthography. Here the interest is word spelling and the alphabet—a word that itself comes from the first two letters of the Greek alphabet, *alpha* and *beta*. Our Roman alphabet of twenty-six letters has done the job for the last millennium, with a few additions, like "j," and a few losses, like "ð."

The study of these changes has benefited from the availability of historical documents. They help explain such odd spellings as "debt," "Thomas," "sugar," and "gherkin," and they show that all the letters of "knight" used to be pronounced. Comparative orthography explores how languages with the same alphabet use it differently. The letter z is rare in English and our Scrabble game awards ten points for using the z tile. There are many more z tiles in a Polish Scrabble game, but using a z yields only one point!

The orthography of English isn't static even today. We're still experimenting with changes. Yahoo!, an Internet computer services company based in Santa Clara, California, incorporated with an exclamation point as part of its name. E-mail suggests that ☺ is making a run for election to our system of writing. The period has found new life now that "dot com" is part of everyone's vocabulary. Companies like eTrade and eBay are capitalizing medial letters. Against the rules, you say? What about McGinty? Or the original Gaelic spelling of Hegarty, OhEigeartaigh. Meanwhile, Prince created his own orthographic innovation. Spelling, stuck with a bad rap from our elementary school quiz days, still manages to reflect all the flexibility, absorbency, and vitality of language.

PHONOLOGY

More than history, the study of language is a study of complex systems that create meaning. Phonetics and phonology are two such systems. While the International Phonetic Alphabet offers a systematic way of transcribing the sounds of a language, it isn't the whole story. A whole battery of features is needed to explain why Fran Drescher sounds different from William F. Buckley. For example, consider "hello." This word emerged in the 1880s to accommodate the business of answering the telephone. Other languages may have borrowed our word: the Spanish say "*hola*," the French, "*allo*." But when and how did "hello" come to mean "pay attention, you jerk"? Phonologists can describe the changes in pitch, stress, and juncture that create this meaning; etymologists might be able to determine where and when the change occurred. Similar sound features allow "excuse me" to mean both "I beg your pardon" and also "Who the hell do you think you are, anyway?" But why do we always say "mergers and acquisitions," "oil and gas," and "money and banking"? Rules of rhythm and stress influence these sequences. The expletive infix rule, for example, designates where in a multisyllable word you can place your discontent: "Phila-fucking-delphia" works but clearly both "Phil-fucking-adelphia" or "Philadel-fucking-ia" don't. Tradition has something to do with it, but phonology and prosody play their parts (and the syllable of primary stress). The sound systems at work in all these examples are regular, predictable, and can be studied.

MORPHOLOGY

Drugstore.com not only has its own special punctuation, it's got disintermediation, business done without middlemen. The word "disintermediation" derives from "intermediate," with an add-on at each end ("dis" and "tion"). It's been hanging around the mortgage business for a while, but my spell-checker doesn't know it yet. Disintermediation offers an introduction to the field of linguistics called morphology, the study of word structure.

Words are born, grow, and die in a variety of ways. Ebitda (earnings before interest, taxes, depreciation, and amortization) is an acronym created by the same process seen in words like NASA, OPEC, and AIDS—words made from the initial letters of a longer phrase. Those soccer team nicknames even follow standard rules for word creation (JD, for example, follows the acronym pattern and O-dog and Greener demonstrate consistent patterns of word formation as well). Ad agencies spend millions on morphology, although they don't call it that. Previa, Viagra, Vaio, and Palm Pilot were created with marketing in mind. Although the Nova had to be re-named in Spanish-speaking countries where the connotation would be "no va" ("doesn't go") rather than "new."

Interestingly, we accept and easily integrate all these different types of additions. The greasy paper facsimile that came through the phone line quickly became a fax. Noun to verb in no time; we immediately knew how to conjugate it. We were all faxing. Some documents just weren't faxable. As we add, transform, recycle, borrow, and morph words to match new products, circumstances, and events, we integrate them according to the system of our language. Sentences like these follow the rules:

He flied out to center.
Look at all the different kinds of Walkmans.
We need a heads-up on that.
That's the 411. Here's the spin.

SYNTAX

Syntax, the analysis of sentences, looks like a page from your high school chemistry text. Syntactic analysis breaks down sentences and studies the parts. Syntax is part of how we understand grammar and part of how we derive meaning. Syntax, the deep structure and the surface structure of sentences, is the basis for claims of the universality of grammar. Tree structures allow linguists to graphically represent the real and the mental organization of a sentence.

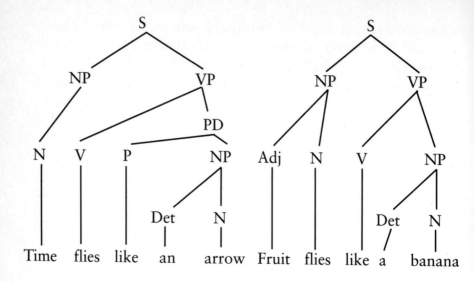

SEMANTICS

In 1980 John Ciardi and Miller Williams published a literature anthology entitled *How Does a Poem Mean.* The clever title highlighted the complex set of factors that create meaning. Semantics is the study of meaning. Now this should be easy, right? Just look up the words in the dictionary. But not so fast. We already know that some things aren't going to be there. And many that appear are hard to define. When an economist predicts a bull market, even if I can find "bull market" under "b," should I count on a 50 percent increase in my mutual fund or a 10 percent increase? Many different patterns might be termed a bull market, maybe even a market that didn't grow.

"Bull market" is a fuzzy concept. Although "dead" or "raining" or "pregnant" seem less susceptible to misinterpretation than "successful," "young," or "early," most words are only a rough match for what they're meant to capture. Ask a teenager what "hook up" means if you need a further example of fuzziness. Apparently, even "had sex with that woman" is a fuzzy concept. Because most words are, to some extent, fuzzy concepts, linguistic experts often consult on trial teams and in legal cases. Actually, doctors are finding even "dead" needs to be defined in the courts. When we try to put our thoughts into words, the fit isn't perfect. The map is never really the place.

Consider these two sentences:

The army officer handed the civilian his papers.
The army officer handed the civilian his gun.

Although these two sentences are remarkably similar, context establishes meaning. The "his" in the first sentence seems to refer to the civilian. In the second sentence, it seems to refer to the officer. Rules of usage attempt to prevent genuine confusion or inadvertent hilarity: "I have discussed your proposal to fill the drainage ditches with my clients."

What we know and what we expect clearly influences understanding. That is one of the key claims of this book. Consider, for example, the powerful conventions of conversational exchange:

Ellen: Is this company going to show profits in the fourth quarter?
Phil: I need to look at the environmental impact statement.

If these two statements occur sequentially in a real conversation, the questioner will assume that the response represents an answer. Phil isn't going to be able to say anything about profits until he's done some homework. Ellen understands that before profits can be assessed, the company's environmental compliance will be researched. But there are limits to the convention:

Ellen: Is this company going to show profits in the fourth quarter?
Phil: I need to look in the closet.

This is a bit of a stretch, but Ellen might assume that somehow this is a relevant response.

Ellen: Is this company going to show profits in the fourth
  quarter?
Phil: My mother's maiden name is Mary.

This response would raise eyebrows; it violates the limits of
response within the conversational convention.

The conventions of conversation vary from culture to culture and even from speaker to speaker. One person may apply
a shared maxim in a different manner (how long an answer to
give to a question, for example) or may fail to identify or
choose to ignore the conventions of the moment. A Realtor's
answer to "Does that fireplace work?" is a good example. "To
the best of my knowledge" does not answer the question. It
isn't false but it doesn't help you decide whether to lay in fire-
wood or not. The respondent is intentionally ignoring the
thrust of the question because he may not know the answer or
he may not want you to know the answer. But the complexities of all communication are increased by conversational conventions—the degree of directness, the length of pauses, the
body language, and the eye contact.

Semantics studies all the factors that contribute to meaning
and reveals how complicated is the game called communication.
It is remarkable that communication happens at all. How fasci-
nating and optimistic we are, chattering on all day, sure we'll be
understood.

OTHER LANGUAGES

If you've tried to explain to your spell-checker program why
you don't need a question mark at the end of "Whoso would
be a man, must be a nonconformist," you already know that
machines don't really "understand" language. But they are trying to. Computational linguistics uses computers to study language, to solve problems, or to answer questions about
language through the observation of computer models. And
every few months, another chess-playing or voice-activated

computer is featured in the press. In his novel *Galatea 2.2,* Richard Powers imagines the construction of a computer whose networks of back propagation would allow it to interpret Wordsworth. The size of the challenge slowly dawns on Powers's characters:

> We could try to feed it algorithms for everything. There are only slightly more of them than there are particles in the universe. It would be like building a heart molecule by molecule. And we'd still have a hell of an indexing and retrieval problem at the end. Even then talking to such a decision tree would be like talking to a shopping list. It'd never get any smarter than a low-ranking government bureaucrat.

Seven implementations later, the experiment still makes nothing but hilarious chaos out of the input sentence "The missionary was prepared to serve."

Unlike the average five-year-old, computers must be programmed for every task. Shown an unfamiliar object and told it is a "wug," five-year-olds immediately call two such things "wugs." Computers have to be taught each plural, programmed for every rule we know instinctively. There's a computer in Texas that is still trying to learn all it needs to know in order to read and understand the preschool book *Spot Goes to a Birthday Party*!

Computer languages do, however, operate on something like the principles of human language. Problems of computational languages can even mimic problems in historical linguistics. Experts in moribund computer languages like Cobol and Pascal rescued banks, data storage, and government systems from the Y2K problem. Like the last living speaker of Old Bulgarian or Cornish, these people held a body of information that was hard to duplicate once they left the workforce. Aging programmers and experts from Russia (where some of these systems aren't yet outdated) offered expertise we suddenly discovered we needed.

Even the study of animal languages offers deeper understanding of human communication. Scientists who study dolphins, whales, and chimps wonder how one species came to have such a sophisticated evolutionary advantage. Are we in fact the only species with that advantage?

NEUROBIOLOGY

Neurobiology and language studies share the benefits of recent developments in MRIs that allow researchers to observe brain activity as people speak. Electrical activity and glucose production in the brains of healthy people have shown, for exam-

ple, that the same area of the brain is active when a speaker says "I pledge allegiance to the flag" as when a signer speaking to a deaf person signs that same phrase. How does the brain instantly know the answer to the question "Do you know the word 'brant'?" Most people can answer that question in one second. No computer can scan so large a database as quickly or as accurately.

Where information is stored and how it is retrieved interests Columbia University psychology professor Robert Kraus, whose research suggests hand motions and gestures help a speaker formulate what she's trying to say. Kraus believes gestures "help people retrieve elusive words from their memory." The mechanism seems to work most effectively for words with a spatial element (under, above) and for words related to motion. If your boss left your important papers either under her blotter or over on the credenza, her hand gestures may be retrieving their location rather than shooing you out the door! Language overlaps, then, with biology. Speech is the result of something going on in the brain *and* things going on in the rest of the body's systems.

How we integrate all that we hear with all that we know, see, and sense is miraculous. All the features and factors discussed in this chapter are part of every conversation we hold. We do it all quite unconsciously. Only occasionally do sentences lead us astray: "Outside of a dog, a book is man's best friend. Inside of a dog, it's too dark to read." Where we don't hear clear sense, we make half sense (all those cute stories about "Give us this day our jelly bread"). Some of the time, things are too complicated:

First old man: "It's windy today."
Second old man: "No, it's Thursday."
Third old man: "Me, too. Let's get a beer."

Most of the time, for all its complexity, communication works pretty well. The rest of the time, a beer is a good idea.

This book has presented language study as a social science rather than as a branch of history, computing, biology, or mathematics. What should be apparent, however, is that all the elements of language study interact. Etymology and morphology together explain "fax." Semantics and sociolinguistics account for "phat." Semantics and convention play a role when Ellen asks Phil about profits. Because the preceding chapters have treated only a small and changing section of language conventions in the subset of the sociology of language, I mention these other areas to show how large the field is and also how disparate.

Almost every academic discipline lays claim to linguistics for one reason or another; philosophy, mathematics, psychology, sociology, neurobiology, computer science, and, of course, the English department all think linguistics belongs to them. The complexity of language—the interconnection of sound, syntax, semantics, psychology, and biology, the infinite accommodations and the amazing amount of stuff we know and don't yet know—may astonish us. It should also make us proud of our innate facility, tolerant about everybody's little errors, and certain that machines will never talk as well as we do.

CONCLUSION

"Everything ever uttered requires cracking."
RICHARD POWERS, *The Goldbug Variations*

The author and critic Anatole Broyard often evaluated a book by asking, "Is this novel necessary?" Broyard posed a question we should ask about everything we write—does this book or article or essay do indispensable work? In writing a book about language in the workplace, I often asked myself the same question: "Is this book necessary?" Ultimately, it was not the research or the reading that persuaded me. It was the people I talked to, the men and women I interviewed and listened to. Over and over, people told me that communication mattered in their work. Over and over, they expressed an interest in their own communication skills, in knowing more about effective communication, and in revisiting and rethinking some of the most common assumptions that underlie how we talk to each other.

First, this book has sought to be educational. As a teacher, I wanted to write a book that would add to a reader's understanding of speech communication. No matter what your other teachers have told you, speaking is more important than writing—and a week-long case of laryngitis is all you need to be persuaded. Few of us have studied language and speech in any descriptive way. We've studied spelling, writing, grammar, and foreign languages, and we come away full of rules and chastened. Speech itself, which comes to us much like walking or sleeping, doesn't require instruction and so all the pleasure of investigation and inquiry eludes us.

Speech, however, deserves a little study. Without a solid understanding of how speech works and evolves, we cannot sort out anything—from what's standard operating procedure in daily conversation to what ought to be taught in our schools. Is "ain't" a word? Is Ebonics a language? Is "I'm like whatever" a sentence? Systematic thinking about speech—especially about our own speech habits—is informative and empowering. We don't need to take advanced courses in comparative linguistics and we certainly don't need to start diagramming sentences. But some understanding of language, its systems and conventions, can make us more aware of the impact of what we say and more sophisticated in our understanding of how we communicate. It can make us more knowledgeable about difference and less susceptible to prejudice.

Language doesn't create our world but language is both mirror and mold. Our speech reflects our world. And it also contributes significantly to how we experience that world. It can be both a social and a political force.

This book has sought to present speech as situational. Education, age, social position, race, values, geography, topic, gender, intention: all these factors contribute to speech choices. All people, men and women alike, shift speech gears when a police officer pulls them over or when a baby is handed to them or when the boss is on a rampage. In particular, I believe, speech style isn't dictated by gender. Doubtless, each of us has a default speech style, a set of conversational habits as comfortable as our favorite sweatshirt. But this style isn't a result of x and y chromosomes. Language is about power. Our sense of our own power in a given situation and the information we receive from others around us about our power determine language choices. We can create opportunity and affect our influence with our words.

This book has also sought to be practical. Once we understand speech choices, once we know that language is connected to power, we can communicate with clearer intention. We can enhance our success whenever talk is part of our work. And we can use language like any other tool—a powerful resource that makes the job easier.

Is this book necessary? I hope so. This body of basic information about language, this brief exploration of the assumptions we have about speech styles, should correct misconceptions and offer readers ways to think about and take control of their spoken language, matching their speech with their situation. I have sought to redirect the conversation about language toward a more accurate picture of what's going on. If language is determined by situation, then it is subject to change. It can be molded to our needs. Women aren't going to be told to talk like men, nor are men going to be told to talk like women. Language from the Center serves one situation and Language from the Edge serves another. Knowing what each sounds like and when it works gives everyone valuable choices.

We all need a battery of tools. With a greater understanding of the sociology of language, we gain control over our expression, and—without ignoring the history of gender, class, race, age—we can make smarter, more powerful choices in the words of work. I hope you have found and will continue to discover ways in which speech can make your ideas heard, your communication effective, and your career a source of satisfaction.

NOTES

Introduction

4 George Bernard Shaw, *Pygmalion* (New York: Pocket Books, 1973), 21.

Chapter One

9 Jonathan Krakauer, *Into Thin Air* (New York: Doubleday, 1997), 23.

16 Erving Goffman, *Interaction Ritual* (New York: Doubleday, 1967), 40.

16 Don H. Zimmerman and Candace West have published extensively on this topic; see in particular "Small Insults: A Study of Interruptions in Cross-Sex Conversations Between Unacquainted Persons," in *Language, Gender, and Society,* edited by Barrie Thorne, Cheris Kramarae, and Nancy Henley (Boston: Heinle and Heinle, 1983), 103–17. Also see William T. Rogers and Stanley E. Jones, "Effects of Dominance Tendencies on Floor Holding and Interruption Behavior in Dyadic Interaction," in *Human Communication Research* 1 (1975): 113–22.

18 Erving Goffman, *Forms of Talk* (Philadelphia: University of Pennsylvania Press, 1981), 18.

19 See Deborah Tannen, *You Just Don't Understand* (New York: William Morrow and Co., 1990), chapter 3.

21 There are numerous studies that show we respect authority. One example is J. F. Dovidio, S. L. Ellyson, C. F. Keating, K. Heltman, and C. E. Brown, "The Relationship of Social Power to Visual Displays of Dominance Between Men and Women," *Journal of Personality and Social Psychology* 54 (1988): 233–42. The cost of claiming expertise has been explored by Ridgeway and also by Butler and Geis (see Bibliography).

23 Robert R. Provine's work with laughter and humor is discussed by Natalie Angier in "Laughs: Rhythmic Bursts of Social Glue," *The New York Times*, February 27, 1996, C1, and in his own book *Laughter: A Scientific Investigation* (London: Faber, 1999). Lawrence Mintz (University of Maryland, College Park) and John Morreall (University of South Florida, Tampa) have also researched this topic.

27 Michael Lewis, *Liar's Poker: Rising Through the Wreckage on Wall Street* (New York: Penguin Books, 1990), 242.

28 Virginia Valian, *Why So Slow?: The Advancement of Women* (Cambridge, Mass.: MIT Press, 1998), 316, 323. See also chapter 14 and S. T. Fiske and S. E. Taylor, *Social Cognition*, 2d ed. (New York: McGraw-Hill, 1991).

28 Studies of expectation and outcome have included a range of subjects, from athletes anticipating their performance in a game to cancer patients dealing with depression.

29 Jack Sattel, "Men, Inexpressiveness, and Power," in *Language, Gender, and Society*, edited by Barrie Thorne, Cheris Kramarae, and Nancy Henley (Boston: Heinle and Heinle, 1983), 122.

30 Herminia Ibarra, "Provisional Selves: Image and Identity in Adaptation to New Professional Roles" (Cambridge, Mass.: Harvard Business School, 1997), 51, 57.

31 Carol Hymowitz, "In the Lead," *Wall Street Journal*, March 9, 1999, B4.

31 Connie Bruck, *The Predator's Ball: The Junk-Bond Raiders and the Man Who Staked Them* (New York: Simon and Schuster, 1988), 213.

Chapter Two

33 Nancy Boardman, phone conversation with the author, August 6, 1998.

39 S. Graham and G. P. Barker, "The Down Side of Help: An Attributional-Developmental Analysis of Helping Behavior as a Low-Ability Cue," *Journal of Educational Psychology* 82 (1990): 7–14.

39 Deborah Tannen, *You Just Don't Understand* (New York: William Morrow and Co., 1990), 63.

40 Michael Lewis, *Liar's Poker: Rising Through the Wreckage on Wall Street* (New York: Penguin Books, 1990), 46–47, 19.

41 Much has been written about the tag question, beginning with work done by Robin Lakoff and including conversational research by Pamela Fishman (see Bibliography).

43 John Algeo, "It's a Myth, Innit? Politeness and the English Tag Question," in *The State of Language,* edited by Christopher Ricks and Leonard Michael (Berkeley: University of California Press, 1990), 447.

46 Herminia Ibarra and Brooke Harrington, "Deference and Demeanor: Gender, Demography and Self-Presentation in Professional Careers" (Cambridge, Mass.: Harvard Business School Press, 1997), 44.

50 Jonathan Krakauer, *Into Thin Air* (New York: Doubleday, 1997), 233.

50 Recollections of Shawn's personality and style of management were collected in *The New Yorker*, December 28, 1992, 134–45. See also Brendan Gill, *Here at the New Yorker* (New York: Random House, 1975) and Ved Mehta, *Remembering Mr. Shawn's New Yorker: The Invisible Art of Editing* (Woodstock, N.Y.: Overlook Press, 1998).

Chapter Three

53 George Bernard Shaw, *Pygmalion* (New York: Pocket Books, 1973), 32.

53 Nicholas Slonimsky, *Perfect Pitch—A Life Story* (Oxford: Oxford University Press, 1988), 144–45.

57 Mark L. Knapp, at Purdue University, researched greetings and goodbyes in *Nonverbal Communication in Human Interaction,* 2d ed. (New York: Holt, Rinehart and Winston, 1978), 211–12.

63 Michael Lewis, *Liar's Poker: Rising Through the Wreckage on Wall Street* (New York: Penguin Books, 1990), 172, 174–75.

66 Fran Lebowitz, *Metropolitan Life* (New York: Dutton, 1978), 17.

68 Robert Frost, "The Road Not Taken," in *Selected Poems of Robert Frost* (New York: Holt, Rinehart and Winston, 1963), 71.

75 Ronald Wardhaugh, *An Introduction to Sociolinguistics,* 2d ed. (Malden, Mass.: Blackwell Publishers, 1992), 11.

Chapter Four

78 W. H. Auden, "The Age of Anxiety," in *Collected Poems,* edited by Edward Mendelson (reprint New York: Vintage Books, 1991), 533.

90 Robin Wagner, "The Gettysburg Experience," in *Books, Bytes and Bridges: Libraries and Computer Centers in Academic Institutions,* edited by Larry Hardesty (Chicago: American Library Association, 2000), 164–77.

Chapter Five

95 Alan Jay Lerner and Frederick Lowe, "Why Can't the English" (New York: Chappell and Co., 1956).

97 Much has been written about acquiring power in the workplace; throughout this section I have used work done by Rosabeth Moss Kanter in the 1970s, particularly "Differential Access to Opportunity and Power" in *Discrimination in Organizations,* edited by Rodolfo Alvarez, Kenneth Lutterman et al. (San Francisco: Jossey-Bass Publishers, 1979), 52–68.

103 Herminia Ibarra, "Provisional Selves: Image and Identity in Adaptation to New Professional Roles" (Cambridge, Mass.: Harvard Business School, 1997), 35.

108 Lorene Cary, *Black Ice* (New York: Vintage Books, 1991), 179–80.

109 Carol Hymowitz, "In the Lead," *Wall Street Journal,* March 16, 1999, B1.

Chapter Six

118 Nicole Harris, "Searching for a Key Called 'Any,' " *Wall Street Journal,* March 11, 1998, B1.

134 Amy Harmon, "Corporate Delete Keys Busy as E-mail Turns Up in Court," *The New York Times,* November 11, 1998, C2.

135 Richard Powers, *The Goldbug Variations* (New York: William Morrow and Co., 1991), 352.

136 Amazon.com internal memo dated October 20, 1998, cited in Harmon, A1.

136 Erving Goffman, *The Presentation of Self in Everyday Life* (New York: Doubleday, 1956).

Chapter Seven

139 "CIA's Gaffe? A Male Failing," *The New York Times,* November 3, 1999, A10.

140 Robin Lakoff, "Language and Woman's Place," *Language in Society* 2 (1973): 45.

141 Deborah Tannen, *You Just Don't Understand* (New York: William Morrow and Co., 1990), chapters 3–5.

142 Margaret Thatcher in her biography, *The Path to Power* (London: HarperCollins, 1995), 295–96, 306–7.

142 Janice LaRouche and Regina Ryan, "The Right Image and How to Get It," *Ladies Home Journal,* April 1984, 50–53.

143 Tina Flaherty, *Talk Your Way to the Top* (New York: Berkley Publishing Group, 1999), 65.

145 Naomi Wolf, "Are Opinions Male?" *New Republic,* November 29, 1993, 20–26.

147 Virginia Valian, *Why So Slow?: The Advancement of Women* (Cambridge, Mass.: MIT Press, 1998), *passim* and 14.

148 Ken Auletta, "In the Company of Women," *The New Yorker,* April 20, 1998, 77.

148 David Willson, *A History of England* (New York: Holt, Rinehart and Winston, 1967), 290.

149 Linda Greenlaw, lecture on *The Hungry Ocean,* Simmons Graduate School of Management Alumnae Association Women and Leadership Conference, World Trade Center, Boston, May 15, 1999.

149 Valian, chapter 7 and 129–30.

149 Lynn Hirszhberg, "The Jamie Tarses Show Has Been Pre-empted," *The New York Times Magazine,* sec. 6, July 13, 1997, 38–39.

149 Rita J. Simon, "Race and Class Drive Most Conflict Now," *Chronicle of Higher Education,* October 2, 1998, B6.

150 William Labov as quoted in Glenn Collins, "Men's and Women's Speech: How They Differ," *The New York Times,* November 17, 1980, C19.

Chapter Eight

151 J. G. Herder in *Sammtlichte Werke,* vol. 4, 472, as quoted by Joshua Fishman in "Language, Ethnicity, and Racism" in *Sociolinguistics: A Reader,* edited by Nikolas Coupland and Adam Jaworski (New York: St. Martin's Press, 1997), 337.

154 Early research on the subject of Black Vernacular English was published by William Labov ("The Logic of Nonstandard English"). More recent work on this subject has been done by Guy Bailey, J. L. Dillard, and Patricia Nichols, among others.

155 John J. Gumperz, "Interethnic Communication," in *Sociolinguistics: A Reader,* edited by Nikolas Coupland and Adam Jaworski (New York: St. Martin's Press, 1997), 395–96.

156 Steven Cushing, *Fatal Words: Communication Clashes and Aircraft Crashes* (Chicago: University of Chicago Press, 1997).

157 Sarah Lyall, "Word for Word," *The New York Times,* February 14, 1999, 14.

157 Interview with Phil Driscoll, April 19, 1999.

159 Interview with Lindsley D. Medlin Jr., April 21, 1999.

159 Barry Newman, "World Speaks English, Often None Too Well; Results Are Tragicomic," *Wall Street Journal,* March 22, 1995, A1, 6.

159 Ibid., A6.

160 Interview with Craig Weeks, April 20, 1999.

160 Interview with Lorrie Weeks, April 15, 1999.

161 Donald Rubin and Kim Smith, "Effects of Accent, Ethnicity, and Lecture Topic on Undergraduates' Perceptions of Nonnative English-speaking Teaching Assistants," *International Journal of Intercultural Relations,* 14:3 (1990): 337–53, and Donald Rubin, "Non-language Factors Affecting Undergraduates' Judgment of Nonnative English-speaking Teaching Assistants," *Research in Higher Education* 33:4 (August 1992): 511–31.

161 Erving Goffman, *The Presentation of Self in Everyday Life* (New York: Doubleday, 1956).

Chapter Nine

165 Jonathan Swift, "Proposal for Correcting, Improving, and Ascertaining the English Tongue," in *The Prose Works of Jonathan Swift,* edited by Herbert Davis (Oxford: Blackwell, 1957), 14.

165 E. L. McAdam Jr. and George Milne, eds. *Johnson's Dictionary: A Modern Selection* (New York: Pantheon, 1963), 28.

167 William Labov, *The Social Stratification of English in New York City* (Washington, D.C.: Center for Applied Linguistics, 1966), 63–89, 455–81; also "The Logic of Nonstandard English," *Georgetown Monographs on Language and Linguistics* 22 (1969): 1–31.

170 Thomas Pyles and John Algeo, *The Origin and Development of the English Language,* 4th ed. (Fort Worth, Tex.: Harcourt Brace Jovanovich, 1992), 68–69.

172 Katharine M. E. Murray, *Caught in the Web of Words: James A. H. Murray and the Oxford English Dictionary* (New Haven, Conn.: Yale University Press, 1977), *passim.*

176 This syntactic analysis was provided by Deborah Grossman.

179 Richard Powers, *Galatea 2.2* (New York: Farrar Straus and Giroux, 1995), 78.

181 Sharon Begley, "Living Hand to Mouth," *Newsweek*, November 2, 1998, 69.

Conclusion

183 Richard Powers, *The Goldbug Variations* (New York: William Morrow and Co., 1991), 352.

BIBLIOGRAPHY

Angier, Natalie. "Laughs: Rhythmic Bursts of Social Glue." *The New York Times*, February 27, 1996, C1.

Auden, W. H. "The Age of Anxiety." In *Collected Poems*, edited by Edward Mendelson. Reprint New York: Vintage Books, 1991.

Auletta, Ken. "In the Company of Women." *The New Yorker*, April 20, 1998, 77.

Begley, Sharon. "Living Hand to Mouth." *Newsweek*, November 2, 1998, 69.

Bruck, Connie. *The Predator's Ball: The Junk-Bond Raiders and the Man Who Staked Them*. New York: Simon and Schuster, 1988.

Butler, D., and F. L. Geis. "Nonverbal Affect Responses to Male and Female Leaders: Implications for Leadership Evaluations." *Journal of Personality and Social Psychology* 58 (1990): 48–59.

Cameron, Deborah, and Jennifer Coates. "Some Problems in the Sociolinguistic Explanation of Sex Differences." In *Women in Their Speech Communities: New Perspectives on Language and Sex*, edited by Jennifer Coates and Deborah Cameron. New York: Longman, 1988, 13–26.

Cary, Lorene. *Black Ice*. New York: Vintage Books, 1991.

"CIA's Gaffe? A Male Failing." *The New York Times*, November 3, 1999, A10.

Coates, Jennifer, and Deborah Cameron, eds. *Women in Their Speech Communities: New Perspectives on Language and Sex*. New York: Longman, 1988.

Collins, Glenn. "Men's and Women's Speech: How They Differ." *The New York Times*, November 17, 1980, C19.

Coupland, Nikolas, and Adam Jaworski, eds. *Sociolinguistics: A Reader*. New York: St. Martin's Press, 1997.

Crawford, Mary. *Talking Difference: On Gender and Language*. Thousand Oaks, Calif.: Sage, 1995.

Cushing, Steven. *Fatal Words: Communication Clashes and Aircraft Crashes*. Chicago: University of Chicago Press, 1997.

Dovidio, J. F., S. L. Ellyson, C. F. Keating, K. Heltman, and C. E. Brown. "The Relationship of Social Power to Visual Displays of Dominance Between Men and Women." *Journal of Personality and Social Psychology* 54 (1988): 233–42.

Eckert, Penelope. "The Whole Woman: Sex and Gender Differences in Variation." *Sociolinguistics: A Reader*, edited by Nikolas Coupland and Adam Jaworski. New York: St. Martin's Press, 1997, 212–28.

Fishman, Pamela. "Conversational Insecurity." In *Language: Social Psychological Perspectives*, edited by Howard Giles, W. Peter Robinson, and Philip M. Smith. New York: Pergamon Press, 1980, 127–32.

Flaherty, Tina. *Talk Your Way to the Top*. New York: Berkley Publishing Group, 1999.

Frost, Robert. *Selected Poems of Robert Frost*. New York: Holt, Rinehart and Winston, 1963.

Gill, Brendan. *Here at the New Yorker*. New York: Random House, 1975.

Goffman, Erving. *Forms of Talk*. Philadelphia: University of Pennsylvania Press, 1981.

Goffman, Erving. *Interaction Ritual*. New York: Doubleday, 1967.

Goffman, Erving. *The Presentation of Self in Everyday Life*. New York: Doubleday, 1956.

Graham, S., and G. P. Barker. "The Down Side of Help: An Attributional-

Developmental Analysis of Helping Behavior as a Low-Ability Cue." *Journal of Educational Psychology* 82 (1990): 7–14.

Greenlaw, Linda. Lecture on *The Hungry Ocean,* Simmons Graduate School of Management Alumnae Association Women and Leadership Conference, World Trade Center, Boston, May 15, 1999.

Harmon, Amy. "Corporate Delete Keys Busy as E-mail Turns Up in Court." *The New York Times,* November 11, 1998, C2.

Harris, Nicole. "Searching for a Key Called 'Any.'" *Wall Street Journal,* March 11, 1998, B1.

Hirshberg, Lynn. "The Jamie Tarses Show Has Been Pre-empted." *The New York Times Magazine,* sec. 6, July 13, 1997, 38–39.

Holmes, Janet. "Hedging Your Bets and Sitting on the Fence: Some Evidence for Hedges as Support Structure." *Te Reo* 27: 47–62.

Howard, Rebecca Moore. Sociolinguistics Bibliographies. 1998. [Online document]. URL: *http://departments.colgate.edu/diw/SOAN244bibs.html.*

Hymowitz, Carol. "In the Lead." *Wall Street Journal,* March 9, 1999, B1.

Ibarra, Herminia. "Provisional Selves: Image and Identity in Adaptation to New Professional Roles" (Division of Research Working Paper). Cambridge, Mass.: Harvard Business School, 1997.

Ibarra, Herminia, and Brooke Harrington. "Deference and Demeanor: Gender, Demography and Self-Presentation in Professional Careers" (Division of Research Working Paper). Cambridge, Mass.: Harvard Business School Press, 1997.

Kanter, Rosabeth Moss. "Differential Access to Opportunity and Power." In *Discrimination in Organizations,* edited by Rodolfo Alvarez, Kenneth Lutterman et al. San Francisco: Jossey-Bass Publishers, 1979, 52–68.

Kolb, Deborah, and Jean Bartunek, eds. *Hidden Conflict in Organizations: Uncovering Behind-the-Scenes Disputes.* Newbury Park, Calif.: Sage, 1992.

Krakauer, Jonathan. *Into Thin Air.* New York: Doubleday, 1997.

Labov, William. "The Logic of Nonstandard English." *Georgetown Monographs on Language and Linguistics* 22 (1969): 1–31.

Labov, William. *The Social Stratification of English in New York City.* Washington, D.C.: Center for Applied Linguistics, 1966.

Lakoff, Robin. *Language and Woman's Place.* New York: Harper and Row, 1975.

Lakoff, Robin. "Language and Woman's Place." *Language in Society* 2 (1973): 45–80.

LaRouche, Janice, and Regina Ryan. "The Right Image and How to Get It." *Ladies Home Journal,* April 1984, 50–53.

Lerner, Alan Jay, and Frederick Lowe. "Why Can't the English." New York: Chappell and Co., 1956.

Lewis, Michael. *Liar's Poker: Rising Through the Wreckage on Wall Street.* New York: Penguin Books, 1990.

Lyall, Sarah. "Word for Word." *The New York Times,* February 14, 1999, 14.

McAdam, E. L., Jr., and George Milne, eds. *Johnson's Dictionary: A Modern Selection.* New York: Pantheon, 1963.

Mehta, Ved. *Remembering Mr. Shawn's New Yorker: The Invisible Art of Editing.* Woodstock, N.Y.: Overlook Press, 1998.

Michaels, Leonard, and Christopher Ricks, eds. *The State of the Language.* Berkeley: University of California Press, 1980.

Murray, Katharine M. E. *Caught in the Web of Words: James A. H. Murray and the Oxford English Dictionary.* New Haven, Conn.: Yale University Press, 1977.

Newman, Barry. "World Speaks English, Often None Too Well; Results Are Tragicomic." *Wall Street Journal,* March 22, 1995, A1, 6.

O'Grady, William, Michael Dobrovolsky, and Mark Aronoff, eds. *Contemporary Linguistics,* 3d ed. New York: St. Martin's Press, 1997.

Oxford English Dictionary (New English Dictionary on Historical Principles). 2 vols. Oxford: Oxford University Press, 1971.

Penfield, Joyce, ed. *Women and Language in Transition.* Albany: SUNY Press, 1987.

Philips, Susan, Susan Steele, and Christine Tanz, eds. *Language, Gender and Sex in Comparative Perspective.* New York: Cambridge University Press, 1987.

Pinker, Steven. *Words and Rules.* New York: Basic Books, 1999.

Pinker, Steven. *The Language Instinct.* New York: William Morrow and Co., 1994; reprint New York: Farrar, Straus and Giroux, 1995.

Powers, Richard. *Galatea 2.2.* New York: Farrar, Straus and Giroux, 1995.

Powers, Richard. *The Goldbug Variations.* New York: William Morrow and Co., 1991.

Preisler, Bent. *Linguistic Sex Roles in Conversation: Social Variation in the Expression of Tentativeness in English.* Berlin: Mouton de Gruyter, 1986.

Provine, Robert R. *Laughter: A Scientific Investigation.* London: Faber and Faber, 1999.

Pyles, Thomas, and John Algeo. *The Origin and Development of the English Language,* 4th ed. Fort Worth, Tex.: Harcourt Brace Jovanovich, 1992.

"Remembering Mr. Shawn." *The New Yorker,* December 28, 1992, 134–45.

Ricks, Christopher, and Leonard Michaels, eds. *The State of the Language.* Berkeley: University of California Press, 1990.

Ridgeway, C. L. "Status in Groups: The Importance of Motivation." *American Sociological Review* 47 (1982): 76–88.

Rogers, William T., and Stanley E. Jones. "Effects of Dominance Tendencies on Floor Holding and Interruption Behavior in Dyadic Interaction." *Human Communication Research* 1 (1975): 113–22.

Roman, Camille, Suzanne Juhasz, and Cristanne Miller, eds. *The Women and Language Debate: A Source Book.* New Brunswick, N.J.: Rutgers University Press, 1994.

Rubin, Donald. "Non-language Factors Affecting Undergraduates' Judgment of Nonnative English-speaking Teaching Assistants." *Research in Higher Education* 33:4 (August 1992): 511–31.

Rubin, Donald, and Kim Smith. "Effects of Accent, Ethnicity, and Lecture Topic on Undergraduates' Perceptions of Nonnative English-speaking Teaching Assistants." *International Journal of Intercultural Relations* 14:3 (1990): 337–53.

Shaw, George Bernard. *Pygmalion.* New York: Pocket Books, 1973.

Simon, Rita J. *Rabbis, Lawyers, Immigrants, Thieves: Women's Roles in America.* Westport, Conn.: Prager, 1993.

Siress, Ruth H. *Working Women's Communications Survival Guide.* Englewood Cliffs, N.J.: Prentice Hall, 1994.

Slonimsky, Nicholas. *Perfect Pitch—A Life Story.* Oxford: Oxford University Press, 1988.

Swift, Jonathan. *The Prose Works of Jonathan Swift,* edited by Herbert Davis. Oxford: Blackwell, 1957.

Tannen, Deborah. "The Relativity of Linguistic Strategies: Rethinking Power and Solidarity in Gender and Dominance." In *Gender and Discourse.* New York: Oxford University Press, 1994, 19–52.

Tannen, Deborah. *Talking from 9 to 5.* New York: William Morrow and Co., 1994.

Tannen, Deborah. *You Just Don't Understand: Men and Women in Conversation.* New York: William Morrow and Co., 1990.

Tavris, Carol. *The Mismeasure of Woman.* New York: Simon and Schuster, 1992.

Thatcher, Margaret. *The Path to Power.* London: HarperCollins, 1995.

Thompson, George, and Jerry Jenkins. *Verbal Judo: The Gentle Art of Persuasion.* New York: William Morrow and Co., 1993.

Thorne, Barrie, Cheris Kramarae, and Nancy Henley, eds. *Language, Gender, and Society.* Boston: Heinle and Heinle, 1983.

Valian, Virginia. *Why So Slow?: The Advancement of Women.* Cambridge, Mass.: MIT Press, 1998.

Wagner, Robin. "The Gettysburg Experience." In *Books, Bytes and Bridges: Libraries and Computer Centers in Academic Institutions,* edited by Larry Hardesty. Chicago: American Library Association, 2000, 164–77.

Wardhaugh, Ronald. *An Introduction to Sociolinguistics,* 2d ed. Malden, Mass.: Blackwell Publishers, 1992.

Willson, David. *A History of England.* New York: Holt, Rinehart and Winston, 1967.

Wolf, Naomi. "Are Opinions Male?" *New Republic,* November 29, 1993, 20–26.

Zimmerman, Don H., and Candace West. "Small Insults: A Study of Interruptions in Cross-Sex Conversations Between Unacquainted Persons." In Thorne et al., 103–17.

INDEX